Google Drive & Docs In 30 Minutes

"I bought your Google Docs guide myself (my new company uses it) and it was really handy. I loved it."

"I have been impressed by the writing style and how easy it was to get very familiar and start leveraging Google Docs. I can't wait for more titles. Nice job!"

Genealogy Basics In 30 Minutes

"This basic genealogy book is a fast, informative read that will get you on your way if you are ready to begin your genealogy journey or are looking for tips to push past a problem area."

"The personal one-on-one feel and the obvious dedication it took to boil down a lot of research into such a small book and still make it readable are the two reasons I give this book such a high rating. Recommended."

Twitter In 30 Minutes

"A perfect introduction to Twitter. Quick and easy read with lots of photos. I finally understand the # symbol!"

"Clarified any issues and concerns I had and listed some excellent precautions."

LinkedIn In 30 Minutes

"This book does everything it claims. It gives you a great introduction to LinkedIn and gives you tips on how to make a good profile."

"I already had a LinkedIn account, which I use on a regular basis, but still found the book very helpful. The author gave examples and explained why it is important to detail and promote your account."

Excel Basics In 30 Minutes

"Fast and easy. The material presented is very basic but it is also accessible with step-by-step screenshots and a friendly tone more like a friend or co-worker explaining how to use Excel than a technical manual."

"An excellent little guide. For those who already know their way around Excel, it'll be a good refresher course. Definitely plan on passing it around the office."

Learn more about In 30 Minutes® guides at in30minutes.com

The home edit : conquering the clutter with style / Clea Shearer, Joanna
Date Due: **26 Oct 2021**

iPhone basics in 30 minutes : the unofficial guide to the iPhone, including
Date Due: **26 Oct 2021**

Laptops for seniors in easy steps : for all laptops with Windows 10 / Nick
Date Due: **26 Oct 2021**

iPad for seniors for dummies: by Dwight Spivey.
Date Due: **26 Oct 2021**

iPad in easy steps : covers iOS 11 / Drew Provan.
Date Due: **26 Oct 2021**

To renew your items:
Go online to librariesireland.iii.com
or contact your local branch

iPhone
Basics

In 30 Minutes

The unofficial guide to the iPhone,
including setup, easy iOS tweaks, and
exceptional apps

Ian Lamont

In 30 Minutes® Guides
QUICK GUIDES FOR A COMPLEX WORLD®
in30minutes.com

iPhone Basics In 30 Minutes
ISBN: 978-1-939924-72-8
Library of Congress Control Number: 2016919736
Copyright © 2016 by i30 Media Corporation.

Cover and interior design by Monica Thomas for TLC Graphics, www.TLCGraphics.com. Compositor: Rick Soldin, book-comp.com

CONTENTS

Contents

Contents

For many people, getting a new iPhone is almost like buying a car. It's not just because the devices are expensive and constantly used. Buyers get wrapped up in the whole experience. They obsessively compare specs, spend hours reading reviews, and even check out people unboxing the phones on YouTube. After purchasing the phone, it's time to customize it… and show off the shiny new toy to friends, coworkers, family members, and any other captive audience!

Even if you don't get excited about a new phone release, the devices that make up Apple's iPhone family are nevertheless impressive pieces of engineering and design. Consider the following features:

iPhone model	SE	6S	6S Plus	7	7 Plus
Weight	3.99 oz / 113 g	5 oz / 143 g	6.8 oz / 192 g	4.9 oz / 138 g	6.6 oz / 188 g
Display	4 inches	4.7 inches	5.5 inches	4.7 inches	5.5 inches
Resolution (pixels)	1136 x 640	1334 x 750	1334 x 750	1334 x 750	1334 x 750
Processor	A9	A9	A9	A10	A10
Main camera (Megapixels)	12 MP	12 MP	12 MP	12 MP	12 MP
Selfie camera	1.2 MP	5 MP	5 MP	7 MP	7 MP
Video quality	4K	4K	4K	4K	4K
Max talk time (3G)	14 hours	14 hours	24 hours	14 hours	21 hours
Storage (Gigabytes)	16-64 GB	32-128 GB	32-128 GB	32-256 GB	32-256 GB

Apple's mobile operating system—iOS—is also well-designed, and comes with new features that extend the usefulness of the device. Imagine paying for something simply by holding up a phone to a credit card terminal, and pressing your finger against a fingerprint reader. It sounds like something out of a futuristic novel or TV show, yet it's possible now for owners of any new iPhone model. We will learn more about Apple Pay in Chapter 3.

There are many ways to use the new phones. Here are some sample profiles of iPhone users:

Renata is a mom by day and a restaurant hostess by night. She uses text messaging, Facebook, and Apple's video conferencing app FaceTime (see Chapter 4) to keep in touch with her friends and coordinate activities for her sons. While driving to work, she plays podcasts on her iPhone, which is connected to her car's stereo speakers via Bluetooth. Once she gets to the restaurant, she goes to the iPhone's Calendar app to arrange her work schedule, using a shared work calendar.

Harlan is a junior at the local community college, majoring in biology. He depends on his large-screen iPhone 7 Plus to keep in touch with class-mates, using social media applications such as Snapchat and Instagram. Harlan also uses the Google Docs app to prepare homework assignments and collaborate on reports—he can actually type using a portable Bluetooth keyboard that he pairs with his phone. Entertainment options include Apple Music and a slew of games, including his favorite time-waster, Plants vs. Zombies.

Corlis works in the finance department of a large retail chain. Her work-issued iPhone comes with the mobile versions of Microsoft Word, Microsoft Excel, and a financial calculator, all downloaded from the Apple App Store. Other apps on her phone include Slack, a group communications app, Wunderlist, a sophisticated to-do list (see Chapter 4), and Dropbox, a cloud storage app that allows her to access and share files saved to her desktop computer. When she is on the road and needs to relax in her hotel room, she switches on an app that plays gentle background sounds such as falling rain and distant wind chimes.

Les is a retired postal clerk and grandfather. He likes to share photos with his family using the sharing features of the Photos app. He is especially fond of the snapshots taken by his 10-year-old granddaughter. For entertainment, he turns to the official NBA app to keep track of his favorite team, and also plays word jumble games against friends living in other states. While having his afternoon coffee at the kitchen table, he will use his iPhone to watch streaming video through the Netflix app.

Tom owns a printing business in his hometown. The most crucial iPhone feature for him is Siri, Apple's built-in "personal assistant" which allows him to use the phone without even looking at the screen (see Chapter 3). Siri can understand spoken commands to get directions to customers' addresses via Apple's Maps app (see Chapter 4), dial suppliers on his contact list, and even compose text messages.

While the latest phones are powerful and loaded with all kinds of capabilities, there is a learning curve. This is especially true for new iPhone owners who have never used a touch-screen phone, or those who are used to models that rely on Android or other mobile operating systems. Even if you are migrating from an older iPhone, be aware that the latest iPhone models handle certain tasks differently. The new iPhones also offer a boatload of new (and obscure) features that need to be explored. While this guide does not cover every feature, it is intended to smooth the learning curve and help you get the most out of your iPhone and iOS.

We only have 30 minutes, so let's get started!

CHAPTER 1

Setting up your new iPhone

Steve Jobs was not directly involved in designing recent iPhone models, such as the iPhone 7. But the Apple founder's touch can be seen in the sleek design of the hardware, software, and various aspects of the mobile platform, such as the App Store. Jobs famously insisted on ease-of-use as a central feature to all Apple products, and made sure that the setup process for new computers and devices was as simple as possible. That's still true of Apple devices today. It really doesn't take long to get up and running with a new iPhone.

If you own an older iPhone, you can skip this chapter, as the onboarding process is similar to what you are already used to.

Unboxing the phone

If you search the Web for "first iPhone 6 ever sold," a video will appear in the results, showing the lucky guy who was first in line when the iPhone 6 went on sale in Australia. Once outside of the Apple Store, he excitedly opened the compact box containing his new phone. The phone suddenly popped out, landing on the pavement and nearly breaking.

Lots of people laughed when the video went viral. The laughter did not last long. Other owners discovered that the tightly wrapped box is primed to send the iPhone flying if it is opened quickly or carelessly. The trick is to slowly open the box over a flat or soft surface to reduce the risk of the phone being damaged.

Once out of the box, examine the phone and familiarize yourself with the basic elements:

➤ Looking at the screen, you will see the *On/Off* button (also known as the *Sleep/Wake* button) on the right edge of the iPhone. If the phone is in "sleep" mode (active but the screen is dark) pressing this button will display the Lock screen. Hold the button down for a few seconds, and you will be prompted to power off the device. Press it again to power on the phone.

➤ On the left edge of the phone, near the top, is the tiny *Ring/Silent* switch. If the switch is toggled to red, the phone will be muted.

➤ Below the Ring/Silent switch are the volume controls. These will work even if something is playing while the screen is dark, such as a podcast or song. They also activate the camera's shutter when the Camera app is open.

➤ The *Home* button is located below the screen. It also doubles as the Touch ID sensor.

On the rear-facing side of the phone are the camera lens, camera sensor, and flash:

The iPhone 7 Plus has an extra-powerful camera with two lenses, which allows for better optical zoom as well as telephoto effects. The results are stunning!

On the bottom edge of the phone you will holes for the speakers and micro-phone. There is also a Lightning connector jack. Lightning connectors are a proprietary Apple technology for handling recharging and data transfer. The jacks may look similar to USB ports found on many PCs and consumer electronics accessories, but only the Lightning connector cable will fit into the jack.

While older iPhone models have a 3.5 mm headphone jack, the iPhone 7 and later models have done away with them. Instead, Apple encourages own-ers to purchase wireless headphones. This change prompted a big outcry when the iPhone 7 was officially announced, with many people pointing out that the wireless EarPods sold by Apple were too easy to lose. On the other hand, the rechargeable EarPods have some very neat features, including the ability to activate Siri with your voice, even if the iPhone is in your pocket!

In addition, the iPhone can also use wired headphones through an adapter that plugs into the Lightning connector jack, or wired headphones that use a Lightning connector instead of a 3.5 mm jack.

Besides the phone, the box contains only a few other items:

➤ Lightning connector cable that connects the phone to a USB port for charging and data transfer.

➤ USB power adapter for direct charging of the phone.

➤ Apple EarPods with remote and mic (older models connect to the 3.5 mm headphone jack, newer models use a Lightning connector).

➤ Lightning to 3.5 mm headphone adapter (iPhone 7 and newer models only).

Even though the phone's battery may still carry a small charge from the factory, it is a good idea to charge it fully before activating the device and completing the setup process. Connect the USB end of the Lightning con-nector to the power charger, and then insert the other end of the Lightning connector into the bottom of the phone. Charging should not take long. In my experience, it takes the phone about two hours to go from almost dead to 100% charged.

Activation steps for a new iPhone

Activation will take 5–10 minutes, depending on how many optional features are activated. The following directions also apply to phones that have gone through a factory reset (see *How to reset an iPhone,* Chapter 3).

Press the Home button or the On/off button to get started. Note that newer iPhone models (iPhone 7 and later) have a non-mechanical Home button that feels different than older iPhones. Owners of newer iPhones will be prompted to adjust the button's sensitivity during setup.

The screen will say "Hello" in various languages, and prompt you to slide your finger across the bottom of the screen. The carrier connection may appear at the top of the screen.

SIM cards

If you see a "No SIM" message, you will be prompted on the next screen to insert a SIM card. If you do not have a SIM card, or it's the wrong size (older iPhones and many Android phones use a larger SIM card) you may need to get a new one from your carrier. iPhones use a *nano-SIM card*—other types of SIM cards won't work.

Inserting a SIM card involves taking the end of a paper clip or thumbtack and inserting it straight into the tiny hole on the SIM slot on the side of the phone. The slot contains a tray that holds the SIM card. Do not attempt to pry open the SIM tray by hooking the tip under the hole—you will probably send the tray flying. Just push in, and the tray will partially pop out.

Carefully remove the tray, and place the SIM card on top of it, metal side down. There is only one way it will properly fit into the tray, so make sure it is nestled in the tray before inserting it back into the phone.

Setting up wireless, location services, and an Apple ID

You will be prompted to connect to a Wi-Fi network, if one is available. Enter the password and tap *Join*.

Location Services comes next. I recommend enabling Location Services, as it will boost the functionality of many services and apps. Later, you can shut down or restrict certain apps from using Location Services (see the section on privacy settings in Chapter 3).

The next screen prompts you to set up the iPhone as a new phone, or restore from a backup.

If you are the owner of an older iPhone, restoring from a backup is an easy way to import the data, apps, and other settings into your new iPhone. There are two options:

➤ **Restore from iTunes.** You will need to connect your phone to a computer running iTunes using the Lightning connector cable that came with your phone.

➤ **Restore from iCloud.** Enter your Apple ID and password, which will start data downloading from iCloud.

Restoring an iPhone from a backup is explained in more detail in Chapter 3.

If you set up the phone as a new device, you will be prompted to enter an Apple ID or create a new Apple ID. You have the option of skipping this step, but you might as well do it when prompted, as an Apple ID is needed to download apps and use the storage and sharing features of iCloud. If you use an existing Apple ID, any iOS apps purchased or downloaded in the past for any Apple device (including iPads and iPod touch devices) will be made available to your iPhone.

After creating/entering your Apple ID, agree to the terms. You will then be brought to the iCloud start screen. You can skip this, but the basic free service can help you save a copy of your contact list, calendar, email, and other data. There is a special section about iCloud in Chapter 3.

Setting up security for your iPhone

Touch ID is also optional, but I recommend going through the setup process to register at least one fingerprint—it will save you lots of time later on when you want to bypass the Lock screen or use the App Store. All you need to do is touch that finger to the *Home* button, and you're in. It's much faster than entering a passcode or password.

You should also create a passcode when prompted—it's an alternative way of opening the Lock screen and using other security-enabled features. The default is six digits long, but you can also choose a four-digit passcode.

After finishing the setup process, you will be ready to start using the phone. The Home screen will already be nearly filled with apps—these are all preinstalled by Apple, and include core apps such as Maps, Messages, and Photos. You can't delete them, and in most cases you would not want to as they include apps that are central to the operation of your iPhone. However, you can rearrange the icons, and group them into folders (please see *Moving, deleting, and rearranging apps* in Chapter 4).

Setting up email

The iPhone is a great device for reading and sending email, thanks to a well-designed Mail app, voice recognition (useful for dictating quick messages) and integration with Gmail, Yahoo Mail, and Outlook. Here's how to set up a new account:

1. Go to *Settings > Mail, Contacts, Calendars.*
2. Tap *Add Account.*
3. Select from one of the services shown, or tap *Other.*
4. Enter the requested credentials. Typically, this will be a username and password, but for some email systems you may need to type other details, such as the incoming mail server. This information can be gleaned from your IT department or email service provider.
5. Select which data you want to sync to the account. Besides mail, you can also sync contacts, calendars, reminders, and notes.
6. Tap *Save.*

You can also change settings such as the number of lines to be previewed, whether or not images should be loaded, and your signature.

If you have more than one email account, be sure to set the default account. This will display as the "from" account when you send an email from your iPhone (you can manually change this in individual messages by tapping the *From* field).

Migrating from Android?

Going from Android to iOS is a bit like moving from the U.S. to England. People speak the same language, but the accent is different and they use funny terms for trucks and toilets.

Here's a quick rundown of what to expect if you are moving from an Android phone to an iPhone:

➤ Basic touch screen motions are similar, but Apple has several new ways of using the screen (see *The iPhone's touch screen,* Chapter 2).

➤ The app stores generally work the same way on each platform, but users must establish an Apple ID to use the Apple App Store—Google Play accounts won't work.

➤ If you paid for an app on Android, and you want to have it on your iPhone, you will need to repurchase it for iOS in the Apple App Store.

➤ You may need to get a new SIM card or go through a special process to carry over a phone number from an Android device to an iPhone. Check with your carrier for details.

➤ Wearables and accessories (such as fitness trackers) may not work with iPhones. Check with the manufacturer regarding compatibility.

For most people making the transition from Android to Apple, migrating contact lists, email, calendar appointments, and other data will be crucial. If your Android phone stores data on SIM cards or device storage, you will want to upload it to a cloud-based storage service that works on both Android and iOS, and then download or synchronize it to your new iPhone.

For instance, instead of storing contact information on a SIM card which may not work on an iPhone, sync the data to your Google account which can then be synced to the iPhone later. Google accounts can also be used to bring over email and calendar appointments to your iPhone.

As for documents, photos, and other data, Dropbox works on both platforms. Install the app on your Android phone, and make sure it syncs the photos and other data. Then, install the app on your iPhone, log in using the same account credentials, and download the files. Dropbox is explained in more detail in Chapter 4.

CHAPTER 2

Using your iPhone: Touch screen basics & primary features

This chapter explains how to use the iPhone's touch screen and the amazing voice-activated personal assistant, Siri. It also goes into the configuration of the Home screen and other important settings.

The iPhone's touch screen

If you are new to smartphones, you may wonder how a device with just one primary button (the *Home* button) can do everything from checking your bank balances to telling your Facebook friends about your daughter's birthday party. The answer: It's all in the touch screen. The screen lets you press virtual buttons, enter text on a pop-up virtual keyboard, and use other types of gestures, including:

➤ **Force Touch.** Pressing and holding a finger on the screen can place the cursor in a document or email, select an area or object, or mark an item for cutting, copying, and pasting. Force Touch can also be used to remove apps from the phone (see Chapter 4, *How to delete apps*).

➤ **Swiping** and **Flicking.** Brushing a finger across the screen allows for horizontal browsing (for instance, to see the next picture in a photo album) or vertical scrolling (useful in the iPhone's browser, if you want to read to the bottom of a long article or page). Flicking can be used in book apps to flip through the pages, and some games even use swiping for special actions such as slicing tossed fruit (no joke—this is the object of a game called Fruit Ninja).

➤ **Double-tapping.** In email, double-tapping text will highlight text and give you the option of copying, cutting, and pasting. In games and other apps, double-tapping might allow certain moves or special functions.

➤ **Dragging.** Dragging is a combination of holding and swiping, and is similar to "dragging" an item with a mouse on a desktop computer. Try it by holding down one of the app icons for two seconds. Without letting it go, drag it to the right side of the screen. The icon will follow your finger and will eventually be dragged over to the next pane of the Home screen. Let go of the icon, and the icon will be deposited on the new pane.

➤ **Pinching.** This gesture is commonly used for zooming in and out, which can be useful for examining photos or maps. To zoom in, place the tips of two fingers or a finger and a thumb next to each other on the screen, and then spread the digits. To zoom out, do the reverse.

Many gestures and touch-related actions are contextual. That means a gesture may be assigned different functions, depending on the app that is being used. Fortunately, some gestures are nearly universal. For instance, the swiping gesture rarely changes from app to app (Fruit Ninja being one amusing exception!)

3D Touch, Peek, and Pop

With the exception of the iPhone SE, all newer iPhones have additional touch screen actions, which Apple collectively calls *3D Touch*. The touch screens on these newer models are able to differentiate between taps, light pressure (*Peek*), and heavy pressure (*Pop*). Peek generally previews content or provides additional options, whereas Pop will open the content.

Here are some examples of how Peek and Pop work:

➤ From the Home screen, light pressure on an app icon will reveal a menu of Quick Action options for that app.

➤ When reviewing the list of email in your inbox, light pressure on a particular message will preview it, while heavy pressure will open up the message.

➤ While browsing photos and videos in the Photos app, use Peek on a single image to open it up for preview.

➤ From your list of contacts, Peek will let you quickly mail, message, or call someone.

➤ In Maps, use Peek to preview a business or organization, share its location, start driving directions, or call the listed phone number (see the image below).

However, there are some drawbacks to 3D Touch:

➤ It takes some getting used to. Press too hard or too softly, and it may not work as expected.

➤ Apple Apps widely incorporate 3D Touch, as do some popular apps such as Instagram. However, not all apps support 3D Touch.

➤ For certain apps, there does not seem to be much of a point to Peek or Pop—for instance, why bother using 3D Touch to preview or open a photo when it is already so easy to use the touch screen to open it?

Nevertheless, some apps are really improved by the addition of 3D Touch, such as Contacts. If you own a newer iPhone model, play around with 3D Touch to determine which apps work best with the new touch screen technology.

The accelerometer

Besides the Home button and the touch screen, the iPhone has an additional hardware element that lets users interact with the device: an accelerometer.

You can't see the accelerometer, but it makes the iPhone respond to tilting and other types of movement. To observe it in action, open the Compass app. After calibrating it, the app will point to the north even if you rotate the phone or change your position. Many games also use the accelerometer, such as racing apps that let "drivers" tilt the iPhone to turn left or right.

Note, however, that not every app uses the accelerometer.

The Home screen

After using the slider on the Start screen, you'll be brought to the Home screen. It looks like this:

As we will soon see, there are several Home screens, but the first one is where most of the action takes place. Whenever the Home button is pressed, you'll be brought back to the first Home screen.

At the very top of the screen is the Status Bar. It shows the type and strength of the carrier signal, Wi-Fi availability, the time, the battery level, and other indicators, such as Airplane mode and the moon icon, which indicates that the phone is using the Do Not Disturb feature. The Status Bar sometimes shows notifications from apps, Location Services, or various system settings.

●●○○○ AT&T 📶 ❄   8:56 PM   ➤ ❋ 88% ▮▮▮▯

Below the Status Bar are colorful button-like squares, the App Icons. Pressing an icon will open the app.

At the bottom of the Home screen is a row of four app icons. These apps always appear at the bottom of the screen, no matter which Home screen is being viewed. For this reason, they are usually the most commonly opened apps, such as the Phone app, the Safari Web browser, and Mail. They can be removed or swapped out using the directions in Chapter 4, *Moving, deleting, and rearranging apps.*

Owners of newer iPhones can use 3D Touch to preview certain app actions without actually opening the app. The actions vary depending on the app. For instance, pressing gently on the phone icon will reveal names from your Favorites list. Gently press other app icons to see what actions are available.

Switching Home screens

Above the bottom row of icons are several small white dots:

These dots show which Home screen you are looking at. There is more than one Home screen, to hold extra app icons that don't fit on the first pane. A single Home screen can hold up to 28 app icons and folders, including the four fixed icons that appear at the bottom of every Home screen.

Demonstration: Switching between Home screens

Go to the first pane of the Home screen by pressing the *Home* button. The first bright dot indicates that you are on the first pane of the Home screen.

Quickly swipe your finger from right to left across the screen. A new Home screen appears. The second dot brightens. There are different App Icons on this screen. As more apps are added, the second pane of the Home screen will fill up. When the screen is completely full, downloading a new app will automatically create a new Home screen.

Press the *Home* button once to return to the first pane of the Home screen.

How to search your phone for apps or data

Quick—Aunt Edna has just texted you, asking if you can play a game of Battle Monkeys, but you don't remember where you put the app. Is it in a folder on the first Home screen, or is it located on the ninth Home screen pane?

There is a quick way to locate apps on your iPhone, without scrolling through Home screens or folders. From any Home screen, quickly drag your finger from the middle of the screen down. Or, from the first Home screen, swipe to the right. The Spotlight Search screen will appear. Type the term for the app or file you are looking for, and the results will appear below the search field:

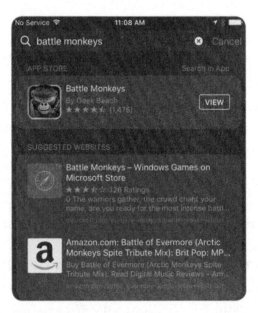

You can also search for emails, contacts, music, and anything else stored on your iPhone, including content within apps. Search results will also show hits from Maps (such as restaurants), Wikipedia, and the Web. These settings can be adjusted in *Settings > General > Spotlight Search.*

Switching apps and multitasking

What happens to an app when you press the Home button and return to the Home screen? Most apps are kept in the background, in an active or suspended state. You can quickly reactivate To switch to a background app, press the Home button twice in quick succession. The Recent Apps view will appear:

Scroll through the list by swiping, and tap once to bring up an app.

If you own a newer model iPhone, there is an additional 3D Touch action that lets you switch to another application: Simply apply pressure on the left edge of the screen, and then swipe left. This will open the next app in the Recent Apps list. Scroll to other apps by swiping. Tap to open a particu-lar app. There's no need to press the Home button!

Quitting apps and shutting down the phone

To quit an app, go to the Recent Apps view by double-clicking the Home button. Scroll through the apps until you find the one you want to quit. Just swipe the app up and it will be removed from the list of apps available in the background. This is a good way to restart apps that are behaving strangely, and in certain cases may slightly improve battery life.

To turn off the phone, press and hold the power button on the side of the phone until a slider appears at the top of the screen. Slide it to the right to power down the phone.

Making calls with your iPhone

Tapping the green phone icon opens the Phone app. Owners of newer phones can also use Peek (with a light press on the Phone app icon on the Home screen) to call favorite contacts.

Once the app is open, use *Keypad* to make calls on the fly, but you have other options, too:

> ➤ *Favorites* shows a list of contacts you have marked as favorite (when editing a contact, scroll down and tap *Add to favorites* to place it on the list).

> ➤ *Recents* will list the most recent incoming calls. Tap the name or num-ber to call the person back.

> ➤ *Contacts* brings up your contact list. If you have added Gmail, Yahoo, or Exchange/Outlook accounts to your iPhone, and enabled the asso-ciated contact lists to be shared, those will show up in Contacts, too.

> ➤ *Voicemail* shows a list of recent voicemail messages. Tap *Edit* to delete specific messages.

After you have entered the number and pressed the phone icon to start the call, the screen will show other options:

Mute. Turns off the microphone. Tap the microphone icon again to turn it back on.

Keypad. Brings up the keypad, in case you are using an automated system that requires additional input.

Speakers. This creates a hands-free speakerphone, useful for driving, simultaneous typing, or other situations.

Add call. Lets you create a conference call by joining other numbers to the current call.

FaceTime. Switches to the FaceTime app, which can be an audio call or a video conference. The other party will need to have a FaceTime account for this to work.

Contacts. Displays saved contacts.

You can also press the Home button to do other things (check the weather, take pictures, play Battle Monkeys, etc.) while you talk. A green bar will appear at the top of the phone's screen while a call is in progress; tap it to return to the phone interface.

Incoming and merged calls

By default, incoming phone calls will cause the phone to vibrate, make a ringing sound, and show the incoming number on the screen (or the name, if the number is already in your contact list). You can use the on-screen buttons to answer the phone or decline the call. You can also press the *On/Off* button to silence the call (the caller won't know this; it will keep ringing on their end).

If someone calls while you are already on the phone, you will hear a beep and the screen will display the following options:

➤ **End & Accept.** Hang up the first call, and answer the second call.

➤ **Send to Voicemail.** The second call will be sent to voicemail.

➤ **Hold & Accept.** The first call will be put on hold while you talk to the second caller.

If you use *Hold & Accept*, you will be shown options to swap back or merge the calls.

Certain carrier networks may not support merged calls, caller ID, or other functions. Check with your carrier to learn more.

Typing and text tricks

If you have never owned a touch-screen device, entering text will seem strange at first. Instead of a tiny physical keyboard (like the BlackBerry) letters and words are entered on the iPhone's screen using a tiny virtual keyboard. The touch screen can also be used to select, copy, and paste.

Step-by-step instructions on how to use these features are shown below. Once you get the hang of it, the touch screen will seem like second nature.

How to use the iPhone's virtual keyboard

Tapping your finger in any area that allows text input (such as the search field on the Web browser, the Messaging app, email fields, etc.) brings up a virtual keyboard, which covers the bottom third of the screen. For instance, if I were to compose an email, I would open the email app, tap the new message icon, and would then tap my finger in one of the available fields (To, Subject, etc.) to begin typing. Because each of these fields requires text or numbers, the virtual keyboard automatically appears.

If you have never used a touch screen keyboard before, it will be awkward at first. To type a single letter, a light tap is all it takes. As you type the letter, a tiny square displays the letter being typed right above the key. This is a visual confirmation that you are typing the correct key.

Other keyboard functions include:

➤ **Deleting a letter.** Press the gray Delete button on the right side of the keyboard.

➤ **Make a letter uppercase.** Tap the shift key (upward-pointing arrow highlighted in the image below) once and then tap the letter.

➤ **Shift.** Tap the shift button once. It will change from gray to white, and the letters will change from lowercase to uppercase.

➤ **Shift-lock.** Double-tap the shift key. It turns white, and the arrow is underlined. Tap it again to switch back to lowercase mode.

➤ **Add basic punctuation or numbers.** Tap the "123" key once, which brings up the numbers keyboard (see screenshot, above).

➤ **Add advanced punctuation and numerical operators.** From the numbers keyboard, tap the "#+=" button.

➤ **Emoji and international keyboards.** Tap the globe or emoji icon next to the space bar.

How to place the cursor to add or delete text

To place a cursor on another part of the screen (for instance, to add or delete text in the middle of the sentence) follow these instructions:

1. Hold your finger on the place on the screen where you want to place the cursor.

2. A magnifying glass appears under your finger, showing the text and the placement of the cursor (see image). Move your finger down slightly to get a better view, but don't let go.

3. Move to the left or right to move the cursor.

4. When the cursor is placed where you want it, lift your finger.

5. Add or delete text as needed using the keyboard.

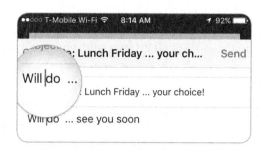

How to copy and paste text

It is also possible to select a word or phrase. Tap and briefly hold a word. The word will be highlighted, with two handles on either side and a menu above:

➤ Pull the handles to increase the size of the highlighted text, or select *All*.

➤ Copy or cut the text (you can paste it somewhere else later by double-tapping where you want to insert the text).

➤ Tap the arrow to see other options, which may include formatting and inserting photos into emails.

Bluetooth keyboards

If the virtual keyboard is difficult to use, and you don't want to use the iPhone's voice-to-text dictation features, you have the option of pairing a Bluetooth keyboard to your phone. Bluetooth is a short-range wireless technology that lets people wirelessly connect their phones to other computers or accessories. Bluetooth keyboards are inexpensive and lightweight, and can easily fit into a briefcase or small backpack.

After turning on Bluetooth on your iPhone (via *Settings > Bluetooth*) and charging the keyboard, follow the manufacturer's instructions to pair it to your phone using a special on-screen code. This only needs to be done once; afterwards the phone will automatically detect the keyboard as long as the iPhone's Bluetooth is activated and the keyboard has power. You can then use the keyboard to type email or use other applications, including productivity apps such as Microsoft Word, Google Docs, PowerPoint, and more. I have heard of students who can't afford a computer using their phone and a Bluetooth keyboard to complete reports and other homework assignments!

Siri and its kid brother, Dictation

Pay close attention. You're about to discover two of the coolest, most useful features on your iPhone: Siri and its little brother, Dictation. Even if you have tried Siri before, read this short section—I guarantee you'll learn some new uses you didn't even know were possible.

Siri is a virtual assistant that helps you find information and data using your voice. It can also launch apps. If you have your iPhone with you and it's connected to Wi-Fi or a high-speed carrier network, do this right now:

1. Hold down the Home button for about two seconds.
2. The screen will turn black, a shimmering audio waveform will appear, and the phone will vibrate, signaling Siri is ready.
3. In a clear voice, say, "Find the nearest supermarket."

Siri will make a tone, and a computerized voice will announce and show what Siri has found:

Results can include definitions, Web pages, maps, and other information. Tapping a single result will display more information.

If you don't see Siri when you hold down the home button, go to *Settings* > *Siri* and make sure it is turned on. You can also change the gender of the computerized voice, as well as the language and even the accent Siri uses. If you own a newer model iPhone (iPhone 6S or later) you can turn on "Hey Siri," which will let you query Siri without pressing the Home button. It will even work if the phone is sleeping!

Siri is not only futuristic, but also cuts down the time required to find directions, set up meetings, and perform many other tasks. Here are some of the things you can do with Siri:

➤ **Call a phone number** in your contact list ("Call Jill Smith at home").

➤ **Check email** ("Check email").

➤ **Compose email** and text messages ("Email Jim Smith"/"Send a message to Jim Smith").

➤ **Post to social media** ("Post to Twitter"/"Post to Facebook").

➤ **Check the weather, local movie listings,** and **sports scores** ("What's tomorrow's weather").

➤ **Review calendars** and **make appointments** ("Check appointments"/"Make appointments").

➤ **Get directions** ("How do I get to Main Street from here").

➤ **Find local restaurants** and read the reviews ("What's the nearest Chinese restaurant").

➤ **Create alarms** ("Set alarm for 8 am tomorrow morning").

➤ **Play music** and **podcasts** ("Play 'Beat it' by Michael Jackson").

➤ **Search the Internet** for information ("What's the capital of Australia").

➤ **Crack random jokes** ("What is the meaning of life?").

Siri isn't perfect. In fact, it frequently stumbles. While researching this book, posing the question "Where is the nearest post office" displayed a local packaging service instead. At other times, Siri may not respond, or may announce that it cannot be used. It also requires Wi-Fi or a fast carrier signal.

Nevertheless, Siri is a huge timesaver, and in recent years it has become much "smarter" about predicting what information users are looking for. Learn how to use it!

Dictation as a substitute for typing

The iPhone's virtual keyboard includes a key with a tiny microphone on it. If you are connected to a Wi-Fi access point or fast mobile network, tap the microphone icon to activate Dictation, which uses the same voice recognition as Siri. Speak, and tap *Done* when finished. It may take a few seconds for the text to register, but it will eventually appear. You may need to make some corrections for special words or names.

> **Protip:** Dictation is so effective that I rarely use the phone's virtual keyboard to send text messages. Why bother? Dictation is so much faster than typing!

The iPhone's cameras

The iPhone's two cameras are marvels, especially on newer models such as the iPhone 7 Plus, whose main camera has two lenses for optical zoom and telephoto effects. The quality of the photos is better than many point-and-shoot digital cameras, and the camera includes advanced features such as the ability to take slow-motion video. Integration with apps such as Messages, FaceTime, Facebook, Dropbox, etc. means that the photos and video are easy to share.

The downsides to these powerful cameras: They will really eat up the storage space on your iPhone. This is especially true of iPhones that come with the lowest tier of built-in storage. Shutterbugs are constantly juggling which photos, videos, apps, and songs to delete to make way for new images.

Offloading photos and videos to iCloud is an imperfect solution, as I describe in Chapter 2. A better option is to use third-party services to automatically save a copy of every photo and video you take. One of the services, Dropbox, is briefly explained in Chapter 4, and I have also written a book titled *Dropbox In 30 Minutes* (see *in30minutes.com* for more information).

How to shoot a photo

It's not hard to use the camera. Tap the Camera icon on the Home screen and press the big button on the screen or one of the volume buttons. The photo is instantly available in the Photos app (see *How to browse photos* in Chapter 2).

There are two other ways to quickly access the camera:

1. **From the Lock screen.** Slide your finger or thumb to the left, and the camera will be available without having to enter a passcode.

2. **From any Home screen or app:** Swipe up from the bottom of the screen to reveal the Quick Options Panel, and tap the camera icon.

You can also adjust the exposure by tapping on the screen to select a point you want to optimize the exposure for. So, if you are taking a photo where the subject is poorly lit, tap on a lighter portion of the photo and the iPhone will automatically adjust the exposure to make the other elements of the photo brighter.

How to shoot video and panoramic shots

Next to the shutter button are options for special photos and videos. Slide the selector to one of the following:

Pano. Take a panoramic shot by pressing the shutter button, and steadily moving the frame from left to right along the arrow provided. It's great for photographing landscapes or other scenes that don't fit on the screen.

Square. The frame is cropped to a square. This is useful for taking square profile photos, as well as for apps such as Instagram.

Video. Taking a video with your iPhone is convenient, but note that the length of the video may be truncated if you don't have much storage space on your phone (this is particularly true of 4K videos taken on models with limited storage space).

Slomo. This is a neat effect for kids, animals, or other moving objects. Press the shutter button once, hold your camera steady, and then press the button again when the activity is complete. The iPhone will take 120 or 240 photos per second to create the slow-motion video, so keep it short. Note that the iPhone also degrades the quality of the video, so close-up videos work best.

Time-lapse. Create a time-lapse video.

Burst mode. To take a rapid-fire sequence of photos, press and hold the shutter button while the selector is on Photo.

Using flash, HDR, and other camera features

The icons on the screen allow access to additional features:

➤ **Flash.** By default, it's set to *Auto*. Tap the lightning bolt icon to turn it on or off.

➤ **High Dynamic Range.** HDR helps the main camera better handle scenes with high contrast, such as a shadowy room with sun streaming through the window. It doesn't work as well when movement or people are in the frame. My recommendation is to tap the HDR icon to set it to *Auto* or turn off HDR.

➤ **Timer.** Choose a 3-second or 10-second delay.

➤ **Switch lenses.** To take selfies, tap the camera icon with the swirly arrows to switch the camera. Note that the camera lens above the screen is not as powerful as the main camera, but for selfies it is more than adequate.

➤ **Color.** Tap the icon that looks like three overlapping circles to choose simple filters for your shots, including black & white.

➤ **Live Photo.** The nested circles icon indicates whether the *Live Photo* feature is activated.

Live Photos

Newer iPhone models have a special camera feature called Live Photos. The camera automatically takes short video clips every time a photo is taken. The photos can be displayed as still photos. But by pressing on the phone's 3D Touch Display, the photos will animate for a second or two. Live Photos can be used as Lock screen backgrounds, and can also be opened on older iPhones, Macs, and the Apple Watch.

The feature is nice, particularly for photos of kids or scenes with some movement. It is somewhat pointless for photos of landscapes or stills.

A big drawback of Live Photos is they take up about twice as much storage space as a still photo. To disable the feature, open the Camera app and touch the nested circles icon next to the timer. If the icon is yellow, Live Photos is on. If it is white, the feature is off.

Organizing photos and videos with the Photos app

The iPhone comes with a Photos app that not only organizes photos, but also provides simple editing and sharing capabilities. The iOS Photos app is integrated with the macOS Photos application and iCloud, so photos you take on your phone will appear on your Mac and other iOS devices using the same Apple ID. In addition, albums created on a Mac or iPad will appear on the iPhone when you browse the Photos app.

How to browse photos

Open the app. There are several views of the photos stored on the iPhone. Tap the **Photos** icon, and you will be presented with *Collections* based on dates and locations (new photos and videos are automatically tagged with geographic information).

Tap a photo to view it. For a landscape photo, hold the iPhone horizontally to see it full screen. Swipe left to see the previous photo in the album, right to see the next photo. Owners of newer model iPhones can use 3D Touch to preview photos—just lightly press a thumbnail while browsing.

Use the icons at the bottom of the screen to sort and view your photos. Options include:

Photos. Browse according to *Collections* (a group of photos from a particular location and time) or by year.

Memories. This feature creates a short movie based on groups of photos. The "memories" are a neat way to present a slideshow of photos to friends, colleagues, or relatives. An individual memory is automatically curated based on the photos in your collections, although it's possible to change the photos by tapping *Select*. To change the music, duration, or other settings, start the memory and then tap it to display various options. Note that if you are using iCloud to store photos, it may take some time to download them before they can be displayed in a memory.

Shared. This view includes photos shared with you or shared by you via iCloud Photo Sharing. It does not include photos that are shared using Email, social networks, or other methods. iCloud Photo Sharing is explained in more detail below.

Albums are groups of photos and videos automatically organized by type (Selfies, Favorites, Videos, Panoramas) or your own designations (Mary's wedding, New Year's Eve 2017, Our beach house, etc.). Tap the plus icon at the top of the screen to create a new album.

Notes on using iCloud Photo Library

iCloud Photo Library is Apple's solution to the problem of digital photos and videos taking up too much storage space on iPhones, iPads, and Macs. When activated (via *Settings > iCloud > Photos*) a low-resolution version of the photo or clip is stored on the device. The original version is uploaded to iCloud (Apple's online storage service) and is only displayed if you select it while browsing the Photos app.

There are a few things to keep in mind when browsing photos on your phone:

➤ Tapping on a photo will generate a low-resolution preview while the high-resolution version is downloaded to your iPhone. If you are using a slow connection, the photo or video may take a long time to load—or may not load at all.

➤ Deleted photos and videos are permanently removed from iCloud Photo Library. In other words, you cannot save photos or videos you no longer want to store on the phone but want to keep for your archives.

How to share photos

As described earlier, iCloud Photo Sharing is designed to work with other iPhone users. However, it is also possible to upload images and videos in Photos to social networks or send them as email or text attachments that can be read on any phone or tablet, including Android and Windows devices.

While viewing a photo on your iPhone, tap the rectangular icon that has an arrow pointing up, and various sharing, saving, and printing options will be shown for the selected photo. Multiple photos can be added to the selection:

Options include:

➤ Adding a photo to a shared album.

➤ Sending it via text message or email.

➤ Posting the photo to a social network. Playing a slideshow of selected photos.

➤ Using the photo as your phone's wallpaper (see Chapter 3).

➤ Sending it to a printer (configuration required).

➤ Assigning the photo to a contact in your address book.

➤ Sending or opening the photo in another application, such as Dropbox.

You may also see other Macs, iPhones, or iPads show up in the AirDrop field. AirDrop is a technology that lets people quickly transfer files to nearby Apple devices using Bluetooth or Wi-Fi.

How to edit photos

The Photos app has come a long way in terms of editing options. When viewing a photo, tap the icon that looks like three tiny sliders to perform the following operations:

➤ **Red eye.** Use this tool to reduce or eliminate the red eye effect caused by your phone's flash.

➤ **Instant fix.** The magic wand icon activates a function that analyzes the photo and instantly corrects the exposure, contrast, and other settings.

➤ **Crop, tilt, and rotate.** Tap the icon that looks like a twisting square. You'll be able to crop the photo by moving the corners, or adjust the tilt by spinning the wheel. There are also controls to rotate the photo and use preset crops, such as square or a rectangle set to a certain aspect ratio.

➤ **Apply filters.** Tap the three overlapping circles to choose from various color and black & white filters.

➤ **Adjust color and exposure.** The icon that looks like a adjustable knob reveals settings for exposure, colors, and black & white.

➤ **More actions.** Tap the three dots to open the photo in another photo editor, such as Camera+ (see *review* in Chapter 4).

How to edit videos

The Photos app has limited editing options for videos. You can crop a video by grabbing the sliders at the top of the video, but that's about it.

Fortunately, Apple offers a solid video-editing app for free. Go to the App Store to download iMovie, or try out one of the many third-party apps for editing videos. Some of them are quite sophisticated, and allow users to manipulate audio levels, add voiceovers, and even append credits and other graphic effects.

How to delete photos and videos

While viewing the photo or video, tap the trashcan icon and then *Delete photo.*

To delete many photos or videos at once, open the album or collection and follow these steps:

1. Tap *Select.*
2. Choose photos by tapping them. A checkmark will appear next to selected photos.
3. Tap the trashcan icon.
4. Tap *Delete photo.*

If you mistakenly delete a photo, tap Albums and scroll down to *Recently Deleted.* Select the photo and tap *Recover.*

CHAPTER 3

Managing your phone: From iCloud to system settings

We have covered the basics of how to set up and use your iPhone. Now we get into the nitty-gritty of making it work the way you want it to. We will also cover iCloud, Apple Wallet, and other useful services.

The Settings app and Quick Options Panel

Many of the instructions described below involve accessing various settings, which are available via the Settings app. To make changes, tap the gear-shaped icon on the Home screen.

For several commonly accessed settings, you can also use the Quick Options panel. Press the Home button once, and slide your finger or thumb from the bottom edge of the screen to the middle of the screen. The panel will appear:

Tap the icons to toggle the following features:

> ➤ **Airplane mode.** Disables wireless services, including carrier reception and Wi-Fi.

> ➤ **Wi-Fi** and **Bluetooth.**

> ➤ **Do Not Disturb.** This mode turns off the phone's ringer as well as incoming notifications.

> ➤ **Lock screen.** Prevents the screen from rotating to landscape mode.

> ➤ **Brightness.** Manually adjust the brightness of the phone's screen.

> ➤ **AirPlay Mirroring.** Display your iPhone screen on a nearby Mac or Apple TV.

> ➤ **AirDrop.** Set up your iPhone to wirelessly receive files from nearby iOS or macOS devices.

> ➤ **Night Shift.** Changes the color palette to be easier on the eyes at night.

> ➤ **Flashlight.**

> ➤ **Timer.**

> ➤ **Calculator.**

> ➤ **Camera.**

If you slide the panel to the left, another set of buttons will be revealed to control music, podcasts, and other media content.

How to change the background images

One of the first things you'll want to do after you set up your new phone is change the photos that appear on the Lock screen and Home screen. It's easy to do:

1. Open the phone, and go to *Settings > Wallpaper > Choose New Wallpaper.*

2. Browse available images. Apple provides beautiful still photos and dynamic imagery (such as moving bubbles). You can also choose a photo from the Photos app.

3. After selecting the image, tap *Move and Scale* to change the position of the photo or zoom in.

4. Tap *Set* to finalize the appearance of the photo.

5. You will then be shown options to have the selected image appear on the Lock screen, Home screen, or both.

Once the wallpaper is set, you can adjust the brightness of the screen and text size under *Settings > Display & Brightness.* There are additional settings for the appearance under *Settings > General > Accessibility*—options include larger text, zoom, and reduce motion.

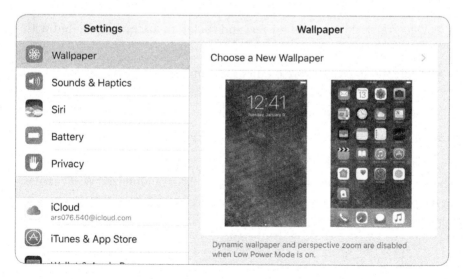

Security and privacy settings

iPhones have loads of security features built into the operating system as well as individual apps and services. The devices are so secure that U.S. law enforcement officials have complained that they can't easily bypass their encryption and other security features.

Here is a list of general security and privacy features available to new iPhones:

➤ Apps are forced to ask for permission before accessing your location data, photos, or contacts. You can revoke permissions for individual apps via the Settings app.

➤ All photos, documents, and other data stored on iCloud is encrypted using the same technology used by major financial institutions. The only easy way for someone to see a photo is if you deliberately share it, as described in Chapter 2.

➤ Mail is encrypted.

➤ When you use Maps or Siri to get directions, trip data is segmented to prevent Apple or other parties from tracking your travel.

➤ The Safari browser on the phone turns off third-party cookies by default, and prevents suspicious sites from loading. Private browsing mode can hide your identity from websites and does not save your browsing history.

➤ Voice-related data used for Siri and Dictation are not associated with your Apple ID.

➤ Apple Pay does not store credit card numbers, and does not pass them to merchants (instead, it uses a system of security tokens and wireless technology to authenticate payments).

➤ Data collected by the Health app is encrypted, and app developers are restricted in how they can use it.

The list goes on, from encrypted FaceTime calls to randomized Wi-Fi access. In the pages that follow, we will explore the security measures that you can activate to make your iPhone more secure.

How to set up a passcode

A basic security feature of your iPhone is the Lock screen, an optional feature which forces you (or anyone else) to use a passcode to access the device. It's similar to using a PIN to open your voicemail or withdraw money from an ATM. For your iPhone, a passcode is a simple deterrent that prevents other people from using your phone or rifling through your photos, messages, and email.

Here's how to activate it:

1. Go to *Settings > Touch ID & Passcode*

2. Scroll down to the passcode settings and tap *Turn Passcode On.*

3. Enter a six-digit number, then re-enter it to confirm. To use a four-digit number or a password instead of a six-digit passcode, tap *Passcode Options.*

4. To change the passcode, go to *Settings > Touch ID & Passcode* and select *Change Passcode.*

Once a passcode has been activated for your phone, turning off this feature will also remove the credit cards associated with your Apple Pay accounts.

How to set up Touch ID

You've probably seen futuristic TV programs that show spies or people on spaceships using hand scanners to access restricted areas. iPhones now include a similar technology called Touch ID, which turns the iPhone's Home button into a fingerprint scanner to open the Lock screen or pay for app purchases.

Touch ID is optional, but it's so much more convenient than using a passcode. Here's how to set it up:

1. Go to *Settings > Touch ID & Passcode.*

2. Enter your passcode.

3. Tap *Add a Fingerprint.*

4. Place a finger on the Home button, and then lift it off. Repeat. As you do this, the Touch ID sensor will read the lines of your fingerprint until it is complete.

While you can use any digit for Touch ID, I recommend using at least both thumbs, which are easiest to use if you're already holding the phone.

Find My iPhone

One evening some years ago, our household was thrown into a panic. Our iPad was missing! Nothing else in the house was gone, so we ruled out theft. I looked in my briefcase, overturned sofa cushions, and interrogated the children. It wasn't anywhere to be found.

Then I remembered Apple devices have a cool feature that lets owners view the location of the device on a map. I logged into *iCloud.com*, and was instantly shown a map of our neighborhood with a dot marking the location of the iPad. That meant it was still somewhere in our house. There was an option to play a sound to help locate it. I activated it. Suddenly we all heard a pinging sound coming from under a textbook. The iPad was found!

Find My iPhone works the same way. It's one of those features that can provide instant relief if your phone is lost or stolen. When activated, it lets you track the location of your iPhone on *iCloud.com* or the Find My iPhone app. It includes the following features:

➤ *Lost Mode* locks the phone with a passcode and a custom message to call the owner (you).

➤ *Activation Lock* prevents anyone else from reactivating a lost or stolen device.

➤ *Erase Data* lets you remotely wipe the phone of all data. This is the nuclear option that prevents sensitive emails or photos from falling into the wrong hands, but also disables Activation Lock, meaning it can be reused or sold to someone else.

Find My iPhone must be activated to take advantage of these features. Go to *Settings > iCloud > Find My iPhone* and toggle the switch to turn it on.

> **Protip:** If your iPhone is ever stolen and you are able to determine its location using Find My iPhone, contact local law enforcement for help in recovering it. People have been hurt or tricked when confronting thieves on their own.

Privacy settings

Modern phones are powerful inventions, loaded with cameras, microphones, sensors, storage, and wireless communications technology designed to make our lives more convenient and fun. But there's a downside: the ability of the phones to perform so many tasks means that we are vulnerable to our private data being shared, stolen, or exploited.

Sometimes we want to share our data. For instance, I like to share photos of my kids with relatives. I let certain apps access my contact lists so I can connect with friends and coworkers who use the same apps. In order to get an accurate weather forecast for my area, I allow my weather app to determine my location from the phone's Assisted GPS technology. But I don't want apps to use my data to target me with advertisements or actively track my location.

Apple generally has very strong privacy policies. For instance, a new app cannot freely access contact information, location data, the camera, or photos—it has to ask for permission first. iPhones also give owners a lot of control over what data is collected, either through prompts ("Google Maps wants to access your location") or *Settings > Privacy*:

➤ **Location Services:** Turn on or off for everything, or make adjustments for individual apps and System Services such as Find My iPhone and time zone settings.

➤ **Contacts, Calendar, and Reminders:** Apps that have requested access to this data (which includes names, phone numbers, and email addresses) can be toggled on or off.

➤ **Photos and Camera:** Social media apps and photo editing apps often request access to your camera and stored photos, but the access can be disabled.

➤ **Bluetooth:** Accessories that use Bluetooth may require installed apps to use your phone's Bluetooth connection.

➤ **Microphone:** These days, apps that use voice recognition technology may request access to the microphone on your iPhone. They include Google Maps (so you can ask for directions) and even banking apps (which may use voice recognition to verify your identity).

➤ **Health and Motion & Fitness:** Under *Privacy > Health*, control the types of data sent to health apps. There are toggles under Motion & Fitness to turn off Fitness Tracking, which uses your body movement to determine how many steps you are taking every day and how long you are sedentary.

Finally, at the bottom of the Privacy settings are the controls for **Diagnostics & Usage** and **Advertising.** I recommend disabling these, as they provide limited benefits to iPhone owners. I also recommend users regularly review settings for individual apps to make sure they have the appropriate access to your data.

How to set up restrictions for children

If you're a parent, you are probably concerned about how your children use smartphones and tablets. Apple gives parents control over certain aspects of their kids' iPhones through *Settings > General > Restrictions*, but in my opinion the controls don't go far enough.

To set up Restrictions, tap the *Enable* link and then enter a passcode. Don't use the same one that's used for the Lock screen, or your child will be able to easily turn off the restrictions.

The panel lets you turn on or off many apps and other features, but these are the ones I recommend you pay attention to:

➤ **Safari.** Turning off the iPhone's primary browser will prevent kids from searching for information or visiting websites. You can also scroll down to *Websites* and restrict usage to safe sites. Apple provides a list (including PBS Kids and *Scholastic.com*) but you can also add your own.

➤ **Camera** and **FaceTime.** If you are concerned about inappropriate photos or video chats, toggle off these features.

➤ **Installing Apps and In-App Purchases.** Control your kids' ability to download games, social media apps, or other unwanted/expensive apps. In-App Purchases allow users to pay for virtual currencies, extra features, or special services, and can quickly lead to lots of charges if not monitored closely.

➤ **Allowed Content.** These toggles let parents exclude explicit songs, TV shows, movies, and apps. For movies and TV shows, you can restrict by ratings, while for apps you can restrict by age group. You can even restrict Siri from searching for explicit terms.

➤ **Allow Changes.** Prevent kids from changing accounts (such as email) or cellular data use. You can also set the volume limit.

➤ **Game Center.** Restrict multiplayer games and adding friends.

Restrictions also lets you control privacy settings related to Location Services, apps, and other features of the iPhone.

What's missing from Restrictions? Many parents would like some ability to control how much time their kids spend on the phone, or how much time they spend on certain applications such as games, social media, or Messages. It would also be useful to have some sort of summary usage report or alerts for parents if usage exceeds a certain level. Unfortunately, iPhones do not have such features... yet.

How to create a VPN connection

A virtual private network (VPN) creates a secure connection between your phone and a remote computer network. VPNs are commonly used in corporations or other organizations where data connections have to be super-secure.

To set up a VPN on your iPhone, go to *Settings > General > VPN > Add VPN Configuration*. You will need to adjust technical settings—including a server address, account, and password—to get it up and running. If you don't have this information, ask your employer's IT department for help setting up a VPN.

Other ways to safeguard your privacy

Set Auto-Lock to 1 minute by going to *Settings > Display & Brightness > Auto-Lock*. This will turn off your phone after one minute, forcing the next person who turns it on to use a passcode or Touch ID.

Use a name for your phone that does not include your own name or other personal details (such as your address). Your phone's name becomes public when enabling certain features, such as Personal Hotspot. Change it by going to *Settings > General > About > Name.*

Wireless

This section covers various wireless technologies that are built into all iPhone models, including Wi-Fi and broadband carrier connections.

3G, 4G, and LTE

As noted earlier, Apple products are built to be easy to use. When it comes to wireless connections, iOS hides most of the ugly networking technology. Assuming you have a valid SIM card, connecting to your carrier is automatic (via *Settings > Carrier*).

iPhones can handle the major flavors of high-speed data networks, which are commonly marketed as 3G, 4G, and LTE. Certain carriers may also offer alternative network technologies for voice or data transmission. The phone will automatically switch to the fastest available technology, and display the connection type at the top of the iPhone's screen.

The fastest is LTE ("Long-Term Evolution"), which Apple claims can reach up to 150 Megabits per second (Mbps). This is comparable to Wi-Fi, and can be used for streaming audio, multiplayer games, and some video.

While 3G and 4G connections have limited ability to stream media to your iPhone, they can handle email, social media, and limited Web browsing. In some areas you may be bumped down to 2G/EDGE networks, which can only be used for voice.

Under *Settings > Cellular,* you will find the following toggles:

➤ **Cellular Data.** Many carriers charge extra if too much data is downloaded to your phone in a given period. If you think you are going to go over the limit or want to otherwise disable data, turn it off here.

➤ **Cellular Data Options.** Enable or disable LTE (useful if you have monthly data limits). *Data Roaming* lets you access other carriers' networks, which can be useful if you are travelling in a region or country where your carrier does not operate. It is turned off by default. If you turn it on, be sure you understand what fees will be charged—almost all carriers charge extra for roaming, and some require their customers to sign up for roaming before they use it.

Carriers have done a lot to build out their systems, but rural areas and even some populated regions have dead spots. Set up a roaming plan if you can, but be careful of excessive fees. Check with your carrier to see how out-of-area carrier connections are billed.

The iPhone's Wi-Fi features

Wi-Fi is a popular short-range wireless technology used in homes, offices, schools, and coffee shops. While Wi-Fi signals can travel through walls and doors, the closer you are to the Wi-Fi access point, the stronger the signal will be.

It's best to use available Wi-Fi networks at home or in the office, as the connection will usually be stronger and faster than carrier signals, and the bandwidth is usually free (meaning you won't be metered for your carrier's data plan). Libraries, fast food restaurants, and other organizations also provide free Wi-Fi. Your iPhone will remember most Wi-Fi connections (go to *Settings > Wi-Fi* to see available connections, or to turn Wi-Fi on/off). You can also use the Quick Options panel to toggle Wi-Fi on and off.

> **Protip:** Some carriers and Internet providers have set up free Wi-Fi access points in public places for their customers. You'll need your account username and password to connect, but it provides an alternative to weak carrier signals or overloaded Wi-Fi access points at the local coffee shop!

Personal Hotspot

One of the iPhone's most useful wireless features is Personal Hotspot, which turns your iPhone into a Wi-Fi access point. This feature is extremely helpful when you are on the road and no public Wi-Fi access is possible for your laptop. As long as your iPhone has a strong carrier signal, the laptop can connect to your iPhone and use the phone's signal to connect to the Internet. Note that some carriers restrict this feature.

Here's how to set up a Personal Hotspot:

1. Go to *Settings > Personal Hotspot* and turn it on using the toggle.

2. The phone will display a "Now discoverable" message and a Wi-Fi password. You can change the password to something that's easier to remember by tapping it.

3. Go to the laptop (or other device you are using), turn on Wi-Fi, and look for the iPhone using the name of the phone (displayed on the Personal Hotspot screen).

4. Connect to the phone, and enter the password provided on the Personal Hotspot screen.

5. When the status bar at the top of the phone's screen displays, "Personal Hotspot: 1 Connection," it's ready to use. Even if the phone turns off, the connection will still work.

It is also possible to use Bluetooth to connect your laptop or computer to your iPhone, but it requires pairing and the range is limited. Stick with Wi-Fi if you can.

Why you should turn off Wi-Fi Assist

Apple recently introduced a new Wi-Fi technology called Wi-Fi Assist. It basically activates mobile data from your carrier when the Wi-Fi signal is weak. Wi-Fi Assist is turned on by default. I can confirm that Wi-Fi Assist can pile on the data charges to your mobile phone bill, as the threshold to activate it is very low.

Fortunately, Wi-Fi Assist can be turned off. Go to *Settings > Cellular* (or, for some carriers, *Settings > Mobile Data*) and scroll down to turn off the toggle at the bottom of the screen.

Bluetooth

Bluetooth is a short-range wireless technology, often used to connect accessories such as headphones and keyboards. For travelers or people on the go, such accessories can help transform an iPhone into a lightweight computer (albeit one with a very small screen).

Bluetooth can also be paired with other devices, such as another smartphone or computer, or even a car's computer system (useful for setting up features such as hands-free dialing). For most devices, pairing takes place using *Settings > Bluetooth*. You will be prompted to approve the connection on both devices. To pair an Apple Watch using Bluetooth, use the Apple Watch icon on your phone.

Four ways to save battery power

Apple claims that a new iPhone can last 1–2 days on a single charge. However, if you like to talk, play games, watch videos, or stream music, chances are you will need to recharge the phone throughout the day.

There are additional steps you can take to conserve battery power:

1. Toggle on Low Power mode via *Settings > Battery* (you may be prompted to do this when the battery drops to a 20% charge). You can also tell Siri, "Activate Low Power mode."

2. Switch to Airplane Mode when you don't need to stay connected.

3. Turn off apps running in the background by double-pressing the Home button and vertically flicking unused apps off the screen.

4. Lower screen brightness via the Quick Options panel.

What is iCloud?

iCloud is Apple's online storage service, built into every new Apple device and computer. It also enables a host of other apps and features, including Photos and various security protections.

On the iPhone, iCloud's features work wirelessly, using Wi-Fi or a carrier network. Once activated, it works in the background—you don't need to "start" iCloud.

iCloud works with specific apps for file storage or transfer of files. For instance, it's possible to set it up so every time you use the Camera app to snap a photo, or add an event to the Calendar app, the data will be synchronized to your iCloud account. This makes it easy to access the files on other Apple devices. It also grants peace of mind—even if your iPhone is lost or broken, you'll still have a backup in iCloud.

iCloud can synchronize the following features:

➤ Photos (see *Notes on using iCloud Photo Library* in Chapter 2).

➤ Mail, calendars, reminders, and contact lists.

➤ Bookmarks from the Safari web browser. Passwords stored in Apple's Keychain (the data is encrypted and cannot be read by Apple).

➤ Apple Pay credit card data (see *The Wallet app and Apple Pay* in Chapter 4).

➤ Location data, which powers the Find My iPhone feature.

Most of these features on your iPhone can be switched on or off in *Settings > iCloud*. Note that some of them, such as paid iCloud storage plans, will require a credit card to be associated with your account.

To learn more about how to use iCloud on Macs or PCs, visit *apple.com/icloud*.

iCloud storage: Free vs. paid

Storage on iCloud comes in two flavors:

➤ iCloud (free): Store up to 5 GB of data.

➤ iCloud Drive (paid): Plans include 50 GB for $1 per month, up to 2 terabytes (TB) of data for $20 per month. These plans are continually upgraded as online storage in the cloud becomes cheaper.

➤ iCloud Drive lets you store any kind of file up to 15 GB in size, including PDFs, presentations, and Microsoft formats.

➤ It's also possible to work on the same file across different apps and devices.

You can upgrade to paid iCloud Drive tiers via *Settings > iCloud*. For people who like to sync lots of photos, videos, or documents to their iPhones, the paid plans are a worthwhile investment.

Syncing & backups

What would happen if someone stole your iPhone, or you dropped it into the pool? Most likely, you would have to get a replacement phone.

Restoring the operating system and apps is not a problem, but getting back your old data (photos, videos, contacts, calendar events) would be difficult, or impossible… unless you have a backup. This section will describe how to create a backup, and how to restore a backup on your existing phone or a replacement device.

This section also discusses syncing, which lets you transfer music, photos, videos, and other content between your iPhone and your computer.

What's the difference between syncing and backing up data?

Let's be clear about the differences between syncing your iPhone vs. backing it up using iTunes:

➤ **Syncing** lets you transfer content and data from your phone to your computer, and also uploads content and data from your computer to your phone. In other words, **data goes two ways.** The purpose of sync-ing is to save new data and content to your computer while uploading new data and content (such as photos) to your phone. The syncing period can be a few minutes long if not much content or data is being synced, or can take 30 minutes or more if lots of photos, music, and other content is being updated.

➤ **A backup** is like a snapshot of all of the data and content on your iPhone at a certain point in time. **The data goes one way**—from your iPhone to your laptop or desktop computer. If you need to restore your iPhone later on or you want to get a new iPhone and bring over the apps, content, and data that you had on your old phone, you can use a backup to do it. Backups will take a long time if there is lots of content, data, and apps on your iPhone.

Syncing takes place every time you connect the phone to iTunes, Apple's media management software for Macs and PCs, or it can take place via iCloud (see below). Backups require connecting the phone to a computer using a Lightning connector.

iTunes is included in every Mac. PC owners can download a Windows ver-sion on *apple.com.*

Syncing/backing up via iCloud: Convenient, but limited

Without getting too deep into the details, iCloud doesn't differentiate between syncing and backing up data—new content and data is automati-cally backed up when the iPhone is connected to Wi-Fi and a power source. However, an iCloud backup is lacking in several respects:

➤ The free iCloud tier has only a limited amount of storage space which is less than the available storage on the phone itself. Users who do not upgrade to a paid iCloud account may have to disable certain types of data from being backed up.

➤ While iCloud backs up most app data, the apps themselves are not backed up. In a sense, this doesn't matter, because the apps can be downloaded again without any penalty. However, if you have a lot of apps to restore, it can take a long time to restore them over Wi-Fi or a carrier connection.

➤ If you have a music collection on your PC or Mac, the only way to directly sync it to your phone is via iTunes. iCloud only backs up and transfers purchased music.

In general, iCloud backups are suitable when you don't have time to connect to iTunes. But for a complete backup that you can use to restore your phone (or a new iPhone) from scratch, connect to iTunes on a regular basis.

How to back up an iPhone using iTunes

1. Connect your iPhone to your computer with the Lightning connector cable and open iTunes, then press the iPhone icon. If you haven't done this before, you will have to follow the instructions after the "Trust your computer" prompts.

2. If you want to back up Health and Activity information, you will need to create an encrypted backup. Follow the prompts to set up an encrypted backup, including creating a special password for the encrypted backup.

3. Once iTunes recognizes the device and syncs, press the *Back Up Now* button.

4. You'll be asked if you want to back up apps, which will store a copy of the application files on your computer. This can potentially take up a lot of space on your computer. Further, as it is not necessary for most apps (you can easily download a fresh copy from the App Store), you may want to skip this option.

How to select content to sync to your iPhone

After connecting your iPhone to iTunes, click the iPhone icon. You will be brought to the Summary screen. You can select content to be synced to your phone or navigate the different content on your phone using the list on the left, which includes the following categories:

➤ **Apps** lists the apps you've downloaded on any mobile device associated with your Apple account. Remove or install apps by clicking the buttons and then clicking the *Apply* button.

➤ **Music** lets you sync your iTunes music collection to your phone. If you have a lot of music, use *Selected playlists, artists, albums, and genres* to narrow down the music that is synced to your phone.

➤ **Movies** includes those you have purchased with your Apple account as well as home movies or video projects that are associated with video editing applications on your computer. Because the files are so large, it's best to select the movies you want to sync, or your iPhone might run out of storage space!

➤ **TV Shows** include purchased programs, such as documentaries or episodes of your favorite programs purchased on iTunes.

➤ **Podcasts** are serial audio programs, including professional radio shows, lectures, music programs, and programs produced by amateurs.

They're great to listen to in your car, in the shower, or while exercising. I recommend managing subscriptions using the Podcasts app on your iPhone—it's easier to use, and new episodes are automatically pushed to the device.

➤ **Books** are ebooks downloaded through the iBooks application.

➤ **Audiobooks** are professionally narrated books, which are good for long commutes or trips in the car.

➤ **Info** lets you sync calendar and contact info.

➤ The **On My Device** list simply shows the content that is currently on the iPhone. To remove a song or movie or book, use the appropriate content area listed above to deselect the item in question.

If you make any changes, click the *Apply* button to start the syncing process. Once the sync is complete, click the eject icon or select *Controls > Eject* from the file menu.

How to restore content from a backup

Restoring your iPhone using a backup means taking an old backup of data—including apps, emails, music, photos, and video—and putting it on your phone. The backup can be from earlier in the day, or from several years ago, or from another device.

During the restoration process, any content added to the phone since the time of that backup will be deleted, so be sure you transfer, sync, or save important data and other content.

Here are the steps required to restore from a backup:

1. Connect your iPhone to your computer with the cable and open iTunes, then press the iPhone icon.

2. Once iTunes recognizes the device and syncs, click the *Restore Backup* button.

3. You may be prompted to disable Find My iPhone. On your phone, open *Settings > iCloud > Find My iPhone* and toggle it off (iCloud password required).

4. A list of backups appears, including backups of other Apple devices associated with the same Apple ID, including iPads, iPods, and older iPhones. Choose the most recent backup and click the *Restore* button.

5. The restoration will begin. Do not unplug the iPhone while this is happening. If you are restoring a backup to a brand new iPhone or an iPhone that has been reset, the process may take a long time, especially if there are lots of apps, photos, and other data on the phone.

6. If you restore your phone from an iCloud or iTunes backup, you will have to redo the setup for Touch ID, passcodes, Apple Pay, Keychain, and other security-related services.

Once iTunes has completed the restoration, you will need to complete a few more steps on the phone itself, including reconnecting to iCloud and verifying the credit card information stored in Apple Pay.

How to manage iCloud & device storage

iPhone owners who take lots of photos, install lots of apps, or download lots of data are likely to receive notifications that they are running out of storage space. It happens to me all of the time, and may happen to you, too, particularly if you own a model with limited storage and use the free iCloud account.

There is no easy solution to iPhone storage problems. It is not possible to insert an additional flash memory card on an iPhone. And, while you can upgrade your iCloud account to a paid storage tier, it will not enable you to cram more apps or data onto your iPhone.

Practically speaking, the best way to create more storage space is to delete stuff from the phone, particularly large files such as videos, photos, podcasts, and large email attachments. This can be done within certain apps, such as Photos and Mail. It is also possible to manage storage space via *Settings > General > Storage & iCloud Usage*.

➤ Under *Storage > Manage Storage*, you can see the available space remaining on your iPhone and select specific apps (and app data) to manage.

➤ Go to *Settings* > *General* > *Storage & iCloud Usage* and select *Manage Storage* under iCloud to manage those apps that save data to iCloud.

➤ Apps can be deleted, which will free up storage space.

➤ While viewing the storage for a particular app, look for the option to delete data. If available, tap *Edit*—a red icon will appear next to items that can be removed.

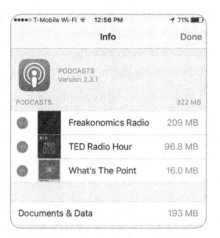

Seven easy ways to free up storage space on your iPhone

The following tips are not a permanent solution to the iPhone storage problem, but may offer some temporary relief:

1. Remove apps that you seldom use. Optional Apple apps such as Keynote and Garage Band are huge storage hogs. Graphics-heavy games are also culprits; some of them take upwards of a gigabyte apiece!

2. Go to *Settings* > *Mail, Contacts, Calendars* and check to see if an individual account (such as Gmail, or a Microsoft Exchange account) has an option called *Mail days to sync.* If so, lower the setting to 1 week or less. Fewer messages will be kept on the iPhone, thereby freeing up more space for other data.

3. Open *Settings* > *iCloud* > *Photos.* If the iCloud Photo Library is toggled on, you will be able to select *Optimize iPhone Storage.* This keeps low-resolution versions of the image on the phone, while saving the high-resolution versions in Apple's remote iCloud servers.

4. Open the Photos app, and turn off Live Photos by pressing the circular icon. This will result in smaller photo file sizes.

5. Under *Settings > Photos & Camera*, change the *Record Video* and *Record Slo-mo* options to a lower quality setting, which will result in smaller video file sizes.

6. Go through your recent photos and videos and select those you no longer want, then tap the trashcan icon. Then, open the Photos app, go to *Albums*, and open *Recently Deleted*. The photos and videos there will be permanently removed after about a month, but you can speed up the process by selecting them and tapping *Delete All*.

7. If you listen to Podcasts, mark old episodes you have already listened to as *Played* (tap the more actions icon that looks like three dots and select *Played*). Then, go to *Settings > Podcasts* and change the *Limit Episodes* setting to *3 Most Recent* (or less) and make sure *Delete Played Episodes* is toggled on.

What is Family Sharing?

Family Sharing lets you share photo albums, ebooks, music, calendars, and other content and data across multiple iPhones (and other iOS devices, such as iPads) in your household. A parent can have control over kids' app and music purchases, people can add events to a shared calendar, and photos can be shared as well. There's even a service that lets you see other family members' locations on a map.

Assuming you are the adult in the family, here's how to set it up:

1. Go to *Settings > iCloud > Family*.

2. You should be labelled as the *Organizer*. Tap your name and make sure *Share My Purchases* is toggled on. You may also need to set up the payment account for shared purchases, using a credit card.

3. Tap *Add a Family Member*, and type that person's name or email address. The name may auto-populate from your Contacts.

4. Follow the prompts to log into iCloud, and tap *Next*.

5. The other family member will be sent an invitation.

Once family members join the shared account, everyone will be able to access movies, songs, apps, and other content ordered by any other person in the family. If you want to hide certain purchases from other family members, you can mark them as private. You can also have other family members ask for permission before buying something—a great way to set limits for kids.

Changing passwords and managing other Apple ID features

Your Apple ID consists of an email address and a password, and is used for identifying your iPhone, setting up iCloud services, and purchasing apps, music, books, and video content.

While it is relatively simple to create a new Apple ID on your iPhone during setup, what if you need to change something? Certain Apple ID features can be managed on the phone via *Settings > iTunes & App Store*. Tap the email address displayed, and then *Apple ID* to see the following settings:

➤ Family Sharing

➤ Country/Region

➤ Ratings & Reviews

➤ Payment Information

To reset your Apple ID password from your phone, go to *Settings > iTunes & App Store > Apple ID* and choose the *iForgot* option. Alternately, visit *https://iforgot.apple.com/* on a PC or Mac.

To change your Apple ID, visit *https://appleid.apple.com/* on a browser. Apple recommends first signing out of all services that use Apple ID, including iCloud, the App Store, Find My iPhone, and the Messages app.

How to control Notifications

Imagine if your bedside alarm clock suddenly began to go off at random times, sometimes dozens of times per day.

That's basically the way Notifications work. A few can be tolerated, but if you turn your back, they'll take over your iPhone, creating a seemingly endless stream of alerts, reminders, and promotions. It's distracting and irritating.

Accessed via *Settings > Notifications* or when apps are first installed, notifications can make sounds or create short messages that appear on your iPhone's lock screen or on a small banner at the top of the screen while the device is on. There is also a Notifications screen, accessed by swiping down from the top of the screen from the Home screen or lock screen (if you see the calendar view, swipe to the right to see recent notifications):

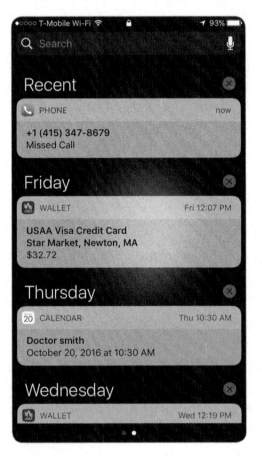

Notifications can apply to:

➤ Incoming emails, calls, and messages.

➤ Activity on Facebook, Twitter, and other social networks.

➤ News, weather, and stock updates.

➤ Game activity and special offers.

➤ Bank, credit card, and Apple Pay transactions.

➤ Flight status and other travel alerts.

In theory, notifications alert you to information that matters. Practically speaking, many notifications range from useless to downright irritating. Remember, app developers generally want you to use their apps as often as possible, so notifications are designed to bring you back. Games and social media are the worst, with some apps issuing multiple alerts per day for the most banal reasons (I'm looking at you, Plants vs. Zombies 2!)

Fortunately, Apple and many popular apps have ways of controlling what comes to you. If you find that a certain app is sending too many alerts, open the app and check the settings (look for a gear icon or three horizontal bars) to see if certain types of notifications can be turned off. For instance, some Facebook notifications are useful, such as when someone mentions you in a comment. Others are unnecessary or distracting, such as birthday reminders for all of your friends. Turn off the ones you don't need.

A second way to manage notifications is via *Settings > Notifications*. Here you can manage the way you are notified (via a message on the Lock screen, a sound, or change to the app icon) as well as turn off all notifications for a particular app or feature. Be careful here—while it may be tempting to turn off everything, you don't want to silence critical features such as incoming phone calls or alerts from your banking app. I also recommend turning on *Government Alerts*, if available—these can contain critical notifications, such as extreme weather warnings.

How to tame after-hours calls

Raise your hand if you've ever been jolted awake by a late night phone call. Raise your other hand if it's been a wrong number, robocall, or crank call.

You can lower your hands now, and consider the options. To avoid these nuisances, some people power down their phones or turn off their ringers before they go to sleep. But what if you want to keep the phone on to respond to family or work emergencies?

Do Not Disturb has your back. This feature, available via *Settings > Do Not Disturb*, lets you silence incoming phone calls and alerts. You can manually activate it when you need it, or you can schedule it to run for a set period every day.

Do Not Disturb also lets you allow calls from people on your contacts, or contacts marked as Favorites. There is even a setting that allows repeated calls to get through, which might be useful if someone is urgently trying to get through to you from a number not on your contact list.

There are some missing features, however, such as the ability to have different Do Not Disturb schedules for different days of the week—I like to sleep in on Saturdays! In such cases, the easiest workaround is to turn off the ringer, using the **Ring/Silent switch** on the left edge of the iPhone.

Accessibility

Hundreds of millions of people across the world live with at least one disability. Apple already has some technologies that can make it easier for people with disabilities to use the iPhone, such as Siri. But there are many other options available, through *Settings > General > Accessibility*:

➤ **VoiceOver.** This feature speaks items on the screen. The speed of the voice and dialect can be adjusted. There are also options for connecting the display to a Braille reader via Bluetooth.

➤ **Speech.** Reads the entire contents of the screen.

➤ **Zoom.** Once activated, double-tap the tips of three fingers on the screen to zoom.

➤ **Hearing Aids.** Settings for Bluetooth-enabled hearing aids.

➤ **Subtitles & Captioning.** Displays subtitles on media content when available.

➤ **Guided Access.** Limits access to a single app, and disables areas of the screen that might cause a distraction.

Other Accessibility features include contrast adjustment, audio settings, and text size.

How to reset an iPhone

Go to *Settings > General > Reset*. There are a half-dozen options:

➤ **Reset All Settings** will reset common settings (screen brightness, Location, Time Zone, etc.) while preserving the data and apps already installed.

➤ **Erase All Content and Settings** is the equivalent of a factory reset—it will completely wipe the phone of data and installed apps, and restore the phone to its factory state with the exception of iOS, which will remain with the most recent version. If you ever sell your phone, or give it to someone else, this is the option you should use before handing it over (be sure to remove the SIM card as well).

➤ **Reset Network Settings** will reset carrier settings and clear out any Wi-Fi networks and their passwords.

➤ **Reset Keyboard Dictionary**. Use this option if you want your iPhone to "forget" names and other words that appear as you are typing.

➤ **Reset Home Screen Layout** will rearrange the icons on your Home screen, and remove any icon folders you have created (the icons will be placed on the Home screen).

➤ **Reset Location & Privacy** sets location and privacy settings to the factory defaults.

When you use any of the reset options, you will need to enter the Lock screen passcode and Restrictions passcode. You will also be prompted to confirm the action (tap *Cancel* if you change your mind), and in the case of a factory reset, you will be asked to enter your Apple ID password.

How to update iOS

From time to time, you may be prompted to go to *Settings > General > Software Update* to update your iPhone's operating system. Make sure you have recently backed up your data via iCloud or iTunes before starting the process. You may also need to plug into a power source if your battery level is low.

It is also possible to update iOS via iTunes, if the iPhone is connected to iTunes via the Lightning connector.

Protip: Major updates (for instance, from iOS 10 to iOS 11) usually entail significant changes to some parts of the user interface. Icons or fonts may change their appearance, or certain features may behave in a different way. Older unsupported apps may also become unusable after a major update. While it is not possible to go back to an older version of iOS once you have made an update, the tradeoff is usually better performance, new features, and (sometimes) some cool new interface elements.

CHAPTER 4

Managing apps

In prehistoric times, before Steve Jobs revealed the iPhone, primitive mobile phones and Palm Pilots ruled the earth. These devices came with simple games, utilities, and other small computer programs called applications (or "apps" for short). It was also possible to buy additional apps, which were usually sold by the wireless carrier or offered by the device manufacturer.

But after the iPhone was launched in 2007, followed by the iPod touch in 2008, the iPad in 2010, and the Apple Watch in 2015, Apple took apps to a whole new level. The company made it possible for independent computer programmers to create powerful apps for use with the touch screen interface and sell them for any price (or give them away for free). Consumers could quickly download the apps from Apple's App Store.

The result was an explosion of apps. Besides the obvious (games, expense trackers, mobile newspapers, Facebook, etc.) a torrent of niche apps that anyone can download is available. They include:

➤ Shopping apps for retail stores and e-commerce companies.

➤ Social apps such as Facebook, and dating apps such as Tinder.

➤ Games, from arcade classics to puzzle apps.

➤ News apps that show articles and videos from local and international news organizations.

➤ Banking apps that let users scan checks and make deposits, without ever visiting the bank or mailing a check to a processing office.

➤ Streaming music and video.

➤ Sports apps for professional teams and fantasy leagues.

➤ Workout apps for custom routines and tracking.

➤ Calculators, scanners, expense trackers, and other utilities.

There are now hundreds of thousands of apps that are actively maintained by the programmers or companies that created them. It is impossible to describe them all, but I have assembled a short list of recommended apps later in this chapter.

Downloading apps

On the Home screen is an icon for the App Store. Tap it to browse apps, or update existing apps. This is what the interface looks like:

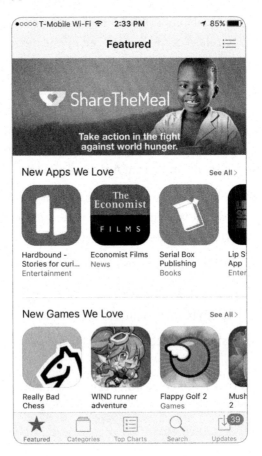

Apple puts a lot of emphasis on games, social networking, entertainment and "fun" apps that skew to a younger demographic. To find other types of apps, you will need to access the icons at the bottom of the screen:

➤ **Featured Apps** are apps chosen by Apple. The focus is on fun and popular brands.

➤ **Category** lets users browse Business, Medical, Navigation, Social Networking, and other categories.

➤ **Top Charts** organizes top apps according to Paid, Free, and Top Grossing (which includes free apps that charge money for in-app purchases). Most top apps in the charts skew toward games and social apps.

➤ **Search** is useful for searching by the name of the app ("Dropbox") or the type of app ("scientific calculator").

➤ **Updates** shows which apps need to be updated. Many popular apps are regularly updated to introduce new features and address usability or technical problems.

When you see an app you like on the App Store, tap the title. You'll be able to review a description, screenshots, ratings and reviews (if they exist) and other information. Tap *Get* or the displayed price to download the app. Regardless of whether the app is free or costs money, you'll be prompted to sign into the App Store using your Apple ID to approve the download. If the app has a price, the credit card on file will be charged. If you do not have a credit card on file, you will be prompted to add one.

Some apps are free to download, but charge extra for *in-app purchases*, such as game credits or extra features.

Moving, deleting, and rearranging apps

Apps can be deleted, reordered, moved to another Home screen, or grouped into a single icon (useful for gathering similar apps, as well as moving unwanted Apple apps out of the way).

How to delete apps

Apps that have been downloaded from the App Store as well as most prein-stalled Apple apps can be deleted from your iPhone by following these steps:

1. Go to the Home screen that contains the app.
2. Hold your finger on the app for a second or two. The app icons will begin to wiggle (see screenshot, below)
3. With the exception of critical apps such as the Phone app and Set-tings apps, most apps will have a small "x" in the upper left-hand corner. Press the "x" to delete an app.
4. Press the Home button when you are finished deleting apps.

You can reinstall an app at any time through the Apple App Store.

How to reorder or move apps

To move an app to another location on the Home screen, or to move an app to a different Home screen, follow these steps:

➤ Go to the Home screen that contains the app.

➤ Hold your finger on the app for a second or two until the app icons begin to wiggle.

➤ "Grab" the app that you want to move by holding your finger down on it until it increases in size under your finger and/or vibrates.

➤ To reorder the app on the same screen: Drag it to a new location. Other app icons will move out of the way to make room.

➤ To move the app to another Home screen: Drag it to the left or right edge of the screen and hold it there until the next Home screen appears.

➤ If you move an app to a Home screen that is already full, the last app on the screen will be bumped to the next screen to the right.

How to group apps

Placing apps into folders allows users to create a box-like icon that can hold dozens of apps. A new iPhone comes with one folder, Extras. But you can also create your own:

You can create as many folders as you want. There are several typical scenarios for grouping apps into folders:

➤ **The iPhone contains too many apps** and/or they are hard to locate on the Home screens. Grouping apps according to categories ("Games," etc.) makes them easy to find.

➤ **A user wants to access lots of apps** from the first Home screen, without swiping.

Here's how to place apps into folders:

1. Move the first two apps that are going to be grouped to the same Home screen (not required, but it makes it easier).

2. Hold your finger on any app for two seconds, and all of the visible app icons will begin to wiggle.

3. "Grab" the first app that you want to group by holding your finger down on it until it increases in size under your finger.

4. Drag app #1 and hold it directly over app #2 until a box appears containing both apps. This is a new folder.

5. Release app #1 by taking your finger off the screen.

6. Both app #1 and app #2 appear in the folder:

Change the default title of the folder by tapping the small "x" next to it.

Other apps can be dragged to the folder, and folders can be moved to other Home screens, using the same methods for apps described earlier.

Pre-installed Apple apps

A new iPhone comes with more than 20 preinstalled apps that were developed by Apple. They include:

➤ **App Store.** Download paid and free apps.

➤ **Calculator.** A basic calculator. In landscape mode, it switches to a scientific calculator.

➤ **Calendar.** A simple calendar app that lets you set appointments and alerts. This can be synced with your Google, Yahoo, and Outlook calendars in the Settings app.

➤ **Camera.** This app takes photos and videos, and allows simple editing of videos (see *The iPhone's cameras* in Chapter 2).

➤ **Clock.** This app shows the time zones of your choosing. Alarm and stopwatch functions can be activated in the app or via Siri.

➤ **Contacts.** This app organizes your contacts, including phone numbers and email addresses. It can be synced with Microsoft Exchange/Outlook accounts and Gmail.

➤ **Game Center.** Game Center connects your Apple ID with game apps, and enables leaderboards and some social features, such as "friending" other players. Some games use Facebook for social gaming, or force users to register an account before they can play.

➤ **FaceTime.** Live video chat with other iPhone/iPad/iPod touch users (see the review later in this chapter).

➤ **Health.** The app gathers health-related data from the iPhone, connected apps, and connected devices including the Apple Watch and various third-party fitness trackers.

➤ **iTunes.** Buy songs and videos with this app. The songs and videos are downloaded to your phone. Unlike iTunes on a PC or Mac, which can be used to buy or play music, the iTunes app on the iPhone is only for shopping. Use the Videos and Music apps to watch or listen to your purchases.

➤ **Mail.** This powerful email program can handle personal and corporate email (see the review later in this chapter).

➤ **Maps.** Apple's Maps app looks great, and is integrated with Siri. An alternative is the Google Maps app.

➤ **Messages.** A texting app that is integrated with your phone number and contact list.

➤ **Music.** The Music app can play streaming music from Apple Music (a subscription service) as well as songs that you have purchased or synced to the iPhone.

➤ **News.** This app lets you select favorite news sources and topics, which are then presented to you in a clean list of headlines and photos. To add a new source, tap *Explore*.

➤ **Notes.** Take simple text notes with this app, using the virtual keyboard or Dictation.

➤ **Photos.** View photographs, videos, and screen captures taken with your iPhone (see Chapter 2).

➤ **Safari.** Apple's mobile Web browser. An alternative is the Chrome app.

➤ **Settings.** Manage hardware and software settings.

➤ **Stocks.** A very simple app for monitoring publicly traded securities and market movements. An alternative is Yahoo Finance.

➤ **Videos.** This app shows purchased TV shows and video podcasts from the iTunes Store.

➤ **Voice Memos.** Record high-quality voice memos.

➤ **Apple Wallet.** This app works with apps from airlines, hotels, retailers, and other companies to display and process coupons, boarding passes, and vouchers. Wallet is also used to change Apple Pay settings (as explained later in this chapter).

➤ **Weather.** A no-frills weather app that automatically shows the local weather if you are connected to a Wi-Fi or carrier network.

Superior alternatives to many of these apps (including Stocks, Calculator, and Weather) can be found in the Apple App Store. However, some preinstalled Apple apps are quite powerful. Reviews of several important Apple Apps are included below.

Four must-try Apple apps

Apple apps range from the uninspired to the brilliant. The list below include several innovative apps pioneered by Apple (Wallet and FaceTime) as well as two other Apple apps that you probably can't live without (Mail and Maps).

The Wallet app and Apple Pay

The Wallet app is preinstalled on all iPhones. It serves several useful functions:

➤ Connecting your credit card to Apple Pay, which effectively turns your phone into a credit card.

➤ Storing movie tickets, loyalty cards, boarding passes, and more.

Set up Apple Pay in a few minutes using a credit card, your phone's camera and either a call to your bank (the phone will dial the verification number for you) or the bank's app. After setup is complete, all you need to do to make a payment is pull out your phone, press the Home button, and hold up the phone to payment terminals that accept Apple Pay. The phone will display the credit card and the amount being charged. Use a passcode or Touch ID to verify the transaction, and you're done!

For loyalty programs, boarding passes, and other member-based benefits, tap the *Find Apps for Wallet* button to get started, or scan a code when prompted. Once the Wallet-friendly apps are installed, they will display passes, tickets, and other information on the Lock screen when prompted by an electronic reader. You can also manually open a pass, such as when you have an electronic boarding pass and need to show it to airline and security officials.

There are dozens of apps for some of the largest retailers and travel companies in the world, including airlines, Starbucks, Target, and more.

FaceTime

If you have used Skype or webcams to make video calls, FaceTime will seem natural. Instead of sitting in front of a computer, the video call takes place on your phone. The quality is great, and FaceTime calls are free, even for international connections.

The first time you open FaceTime, you'll be brought through a setup process:

1. Make sure Wi-Fi is turned on, or you have access to a strong carrier network.

2. Use your Apple ID and password (the same one you used to sign into iCloud and the App Store).

3. You will be asked to confirm whether you want to use the email address associated with your Apple ID to use FaceTime.

The big drawback with FaceTime is it does not work with Android phones or Windows devices. However, you can make video calls to Android and Windows users with Skype's app—see the review later in this chapter.

To make a connection with FaceTime, tap on a name in the list of people you have connected with before, or enter a new name by tapping the plus symbol and selecting someone from your Contacts list. To make a connection, the other person must have an iPhone, iPad, iPod touch, or Mac. FaceTime works best with Wi-Fi.

Initiating a FaceTime call is like making a phone call, in that the destination device will "ring" and a prompt will appear on the front of the screen notifying the recipient that you are trying to connect. If you're making a call, the front-facing camera above the screen will activate and text at the top of the screen will show who is being dialed.

To end a call, press the button at the bottom of the screen.

Mail

It may seem strange to highlight the iPhone's Mail app. It's just email, after all!

But Mail on the iPhone is special. Here's why:

➤ **It's very easy to add accounts** from Gmail, Yahoo Mail, and other providers. Even if you use Outlook at work, you can have it synced to your iPhone using the Microsoft Exchange option.

➤ **It's easier to use** than other mobile or desktop email programs. I've tried Android, BlackBerry, and more PC and Mac email clients than I care to remember. For ease-of-use, the iOS Mail app beats them all. This is partly because the designers have stripped down the program to the most basic and frequently used features, but also because of the integration with other apps (see below).

➤ **Calendars** and **contact lists** associated with Exchange, Gmail, and other email accounts are carried over to the Calendar and Contacts apps. New appointments and contacts entered into the phone are synced back to the accounts.

➤ **Solid integration** with other Apple and third-party applications. For example, open the Photos app and select any photo. Tap the photo once, and then tap the icon in the lower left corner that lets you forward the picture. When you select Mail, the photo is visually incorporated into the message. It's a small touch, but it's helpful.

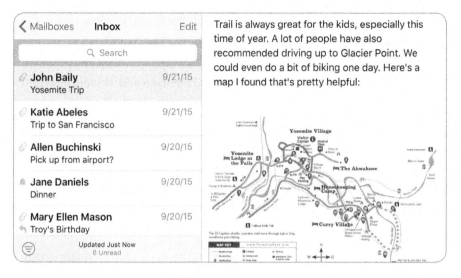

You can add lots of email accounts to an iPhone. Here's how:

1. Try to get within range of a strong Wi-Fi signal—this will help with speeding up authentication and transferring recent mail to the phone.

2. Go to *Settings > Mail, Contacts, Calendars.*

3. Tap *Add Account.*

4. Tap one of the account types (iCloud, Exchange, Google, Yahoo, AOL, Outlook.com, or other).

5. Fill in the email address, password, name, and other fields.

6. Once authenticated, you have the option of turning on other data associated with the email account, such as contacts and calendars. Contacts and appointments from these accounts will begin to appear in the Phone, Contacts, and Calendar apps.

Consider importing contacts, too. Not only will it make emailing easier (the iPhone will automatically complete names and email addresses as you type them) but other apps, such as FaceTime, will be able to access the contact data. This saves a lot of data-entry work.

As stated earlier, Mail is very easy to operate. Here are some key features worth noting:

➤ Tap to open a message. Swipe right to mark a message as read. Swipe left to archive or delete it.

➤ After reading a message, you can reply, forward, archive, or take some other action, using the icons at the bottom of the screen.

➤ To create a new email message, tap the compose icon. Type an email address in the *To:* field, or press the plus icon to add an address from your contacts.

➤ The default "sent from my iPhone" message is appended to all outgoing email, but you can change or delete the signature in *Settings > Mail, Contacts, Calendars > Signature.*

➤ If you have more than one email account synced to the iPhone and want to use a different address in the *From:* field, tap the address in the *From:* field and then use the carousel to select another address.

➤ To attach a photo, press down lightly in the *Body* field of the message until a menu pops up. Scroll right and select the *Attach* option.

➤ Use Siri to check email ("check email") or read the most recent subject lines ("read email). Or, have Siri compose a message for you ("send email to Edward McSweeney").

➤ On the latest iPhone models, use 3D Touch to preview a message (Peek) by holding down on the snippet in the inbox. Open it by pressing a bit harder (Pop).

Maps

Apple's Maps application was released in 2012, and was initially ridiculed for its broken data set and whacked-out directions. When I first tried Maps, it displayed a drivable "causeway" near my house that was no more than a dirt footpath!

Apple Maps has been vastly improved, and is now ready for prime time. Here is a list of some of the most important features:

➤ The dataset has been cleaned up. It now includes business locations, live traffic data (such as slowdowns) as well as public transit information.

➤ Maps is integrated with other apps (such as Contacts and Calendar) to make it easier to find addresses. If you see an address that is a different color than the other text on the screen, tap it. Chances are, the iPhone will recognize it as an address and open it in Maps.

➤ It's even possible to switch to 3D View, which can include buildings and other features in some cities.

But the killer feature of Maps is the ability to get directions. It can even read them out loud while you drive, just like a GPS device.

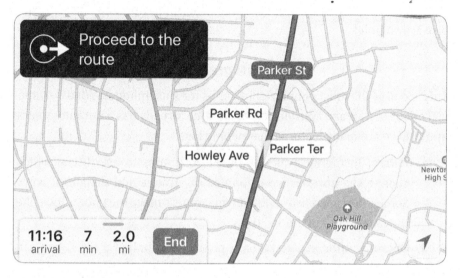

Try it out by following these steps:

1. Open Maps, and tap the compass icon. This will bring up your current location.

2. In the search window, type a nearby address and tap *Search*. The map will change views to a pin marking the destination address, and should display the estimated driving time.

3. Tap *Directions*, which shows the transit time. The map will zoom out, and the preferred route will be highlighted.

4. If an alternate route is shown, tap it to switch to that route.

5. Tap the *Walk* or *Transit* tabs to see routes and estimated times for walking and public transport.

6. Press *Start*. Siri will tell you where to go.

7. Tap *End* when you are finished.

Nine exceptional third-party apps

There are hundreds of thousands of apps in the Apple App Store, which makes choosing favorites really difficult. The apps listed below are useful or innovative, but are not the final word on "best apps." View them as a starting point, and be sure to check out the Apple App Store to see what else is available!

Instagram

This is one of the most popular photo apps for smartphones. What's so special about Instagram, considering the iPhone already has a decent Camera app? There are many features that people love:

1. **Filters.** Instagram was one of the first apps to use filters, which change the appearance of photos in strange and delightful ways. Some filters increase contrast while others make the photos look like they were shot in the 1970s.

2. **Sharing.** After you've taken a photo and applied a filter, you can instantly distribute it via Facebook, Twitter, and other networks.

3. **Viewing cool photos from other people.** You can follow friends, other people, businesses, celebrities, bands, and more. There are some serious shutterbugs on Instagram; seek them out to get a daily dose of world-class photography and be sure to leave comments and likes.

4. **Hashtags.** Instagram supports hashtags—search terms based on words or phrases preceded by the pound symbol, such as #Miami or #chinesefood. This makes it easy to find like-minded people or zero in on interesting topics.

5. **Local photos.** Because so many uploaded photos contain geographic coordinates, by tapping on the location of one photo you can see all of the photos that were taken nearby!

6. **Videos.** Instagram now allows users to upload short video clips from their phones.

7. **Messages.** Instagram has a simple mechanism for messaging people in your Instagram network.

Camera+

This app does exactly what the name implies—it provides an extra-powerful camera app to shoot and edit photos. There are free and paid versions of the app.

If you use Camera+ to take photos, you will find that the icons are easier to understand and the options are easier to access:

➤ Frequently used tools (zoom, switch cameras, and flash) are overlaid on the viewfinder.

➤ Tap the plus icon to bring up the Today Widget, which shows Timer, Crop, Macro, and Burst options.

➤ Tap the menu to access settings. These are extensive, and include toggles for geotagging, quality, white balance, etc.

➤ The icon that looks like a flower brings up the Lightbox, where editing and other modifications can take place. There are a multitude of options, ranging from preset filters to detailed settings for tint, temperature, and blur. It's not Photoshop, but it nevertheless lets amateur photographers perform some sophisticated photographic tweaks.

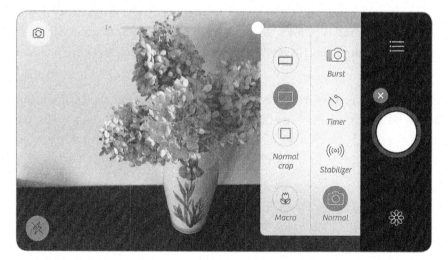

Skype

Skype is a good backup app to have on your iPhone. If you have run out of mobile minutes, you are in a foreign country, or there is some other reason you are unable to use the Phone app or FaceTime, Skype can save the day. Over a standard Wi-Fi connection, Skype lets you:

➤ Call mobile phones or land lines (press the keypad icon).

➤ Take part in audio or video calls with Skype contacts anywhere in the world.

➤ Send short messages to Skype contacts.

Messages and Skype-to-Skype audio calls are free. Other features, such as calling out to real phones, cost money. In my experience, the rates are fair, especially when calling overseas—certainly a lot better than the international rates charged by hotels! Skype has saved my bacon more than once at moments when I've needed to make phone calls in a foreign city to local and overseas numbers.

The video calls are also great, and unlike FaceTime, don't require the other parties to be using an Apple device.

Dropbox

Dropbox is software that makes it easy to store and share photos, documents, spreadsheets, and other types of computer files across every device you own, including Windows PCs and Android phones and tablets. It's very popular, and comes with several gigabytes of free storage. There are paid plans, too.

While Dropbox is primarily used as a desktop application, the Dropbox app for the iPhone is a quick way to access files and folders on the go. There is also a special feature called Camera Upload that automatically transfers photos taken with your iPhone's camera to Dropbox.

Once installed on your device, find the Dropbox icon and tap it. A new screen will appear, which will prompt you to sign in to an existing Dropbox account or create a new one. The first time you activate the Dropbox app on your iPhone, you will see your Dropbox folders arranged in an index. To download and open a file on your iPhone, navigate to the subfolder that contains the file you want to open, and select it. Or, if you know the name of the file but can't remember the location, use the search function to find and select it. Common file formats (such as PDFs, text files, and Microsoft Office files) can be viewed, but not edited.

Dropbox also has a powerful feature called Camera Upload. Once activated from the app's settings, it automatically copies the new photos and videos to Dropbox that you create using your phone's camera. Dropbox grants you some free space, as well—you'll need it, because photos and videos take up a lot of storage space.

The transfer takes place when you open the Dropbox app. All accumulated photos and videos since the last time you opened the app are synced to a new folder called *Camera Upload* in your Dropbox account. This makes it easy to open them up on a PC, Mac, or Tablet that has access to the same Dropbox account.

New York Times

While Apple's new News app is a useful way to browse and read news, sometimes you have to go straight to the source. I've tried dozens of news apps for the iPhone, and there is only one that I still read every day: *The New York Times* app.

The app is very simple. The free version shows a limited number of free articles. Or you can purchase a digital subscription (rates vary) to access as many articles as you want.

One of the most useful features of *The New York Times* app is alerts. Tap the bell icon to set up alerts to appear as notifications on your phone. Breaking News Alerts cover major national and international stories, or you can select Business, Politics, Sports, or other topics.

Epicurious

I used to be such a bad cook, I even managed to screw up a recipe for chocolate chip cookies.

That happened before I got Epicurious. This app, which is basically a giant recipe database, has helped turn me into a passable cook. Epicurious lets anyone, from inexperienced bachelors to serious gourmets, find suitable recipes. No more flipping through cookbooks, searching out a vaguely remembered recipe you tried a few years ago. Epicurious' search function quickly combs through tens of thousands of recipes, based on either keywords ("cabbage") or the name of the recipe ("chicken fried steak"). Recently, developers added visual search options plus cooking timers.

Where do the recipes come from? High-end cooking magazines are a common source—*Bon Appetit* frequently appears in search results. There are also cookbook recipes (particularly for ethnic or regional cuisines) and Epicurious' own recipes. In addition, recipes are rated and reviewed by users, which gives additional data points.

The database is so big, there are usually multiple recipes to choose from. "Chicken fried steak," for instance, generates many results. This means cooks can choose the recipes that suit their tastes, abilities, or the ingredients at hand.

Speaking of ingredients, a very helpful function in Epicurious is the ability to export the ingredients from particular recipes to a shopping list that you can bring with you to the supermarket. Multiple recipes can be combined into a single list.

Bejeweled Blitz

If you are a gamer, you have probably already downloaded some gaming apps that match your tastes. If you are not a gamer, and want to see what the fuss is about, Bejeweled Blitz is a good place to start. It's easy to learn, and the game usually takes less than a minute to play each round.

The game screen shows a grid of jewels. The idea is to use the touch screen to slide a jewel to make a row of three identical jewels. The row disappears, points are awarded, and new jewels drop down from the top of the screen. The game gets a more exciting with bonus jewels, exploding jewels, and awards of bonus coins at the end of each game. Of course, the game gets a little frantic as the timer ticks down.

The game is free to play, but the publisher encourages users to buy more gold coins, which can be exchanged for special jewels and extra challenges. This is how many gaming apps work these days—they try to get users hooked on gameplay, then dangle something special in front of them that costs extra. Resist the urge!

Wunderlist

If you use to-do lists for home, work, or school, then Wunderlist is for you. The free version for the iPhone is a delight to use, and makes it easy to set up lists of... anything.

For instance, I have two top-level folders for home and work, and in each folder have about 10 lists. *Movies* is a list of films that I heard about from friends or saw the trailer for. *Legal* contains a to-do list of copyright and trademark applications and notes relating to ongoing discussions with my lawyers.

Other features include due dates, reminders, the ability to share a list with people in your iPhone contacts, and the ability to email a copy of a list to someone. The Wunderlist account on your phone can also be used to log into *Wunderlist.com* or the desktop Wunderlist app.

Waze

Sometimes I find it hard to believe that Waze is legal. But if you are a driver in the United States (or any other country that allows it), Waze will change the way you drive.

Waze combines social networking features with various navigation aids. The app plots your location on a map and then alerts you to slowdowns and trouble spots compiled by other Waze users. You don't need to look at the app; instead, Waze will announce in a sharp voice:

➤ "Police ahead"

➤ "Traffic jam ahead"

➤ "Vehicle on shoulder"

➤ "Roadkill"

And the amazing thing is … it's almost always right, even when it comes to a flattened raccoon by the side of the highway!

The other cool feature is social-assisted voice navigation. Plug in an address, and let Waze guide you around traffic jams and other trouble spots.

Waze's map view will show where other "Wazers" have left notes or messages about the route ahead. Thus, if you are stuck in a traffic jam that is of unknown length, you can swipe ahead to see where the trouble spot is and what is causing it. The map also shows places to detour, as well as speed traps:

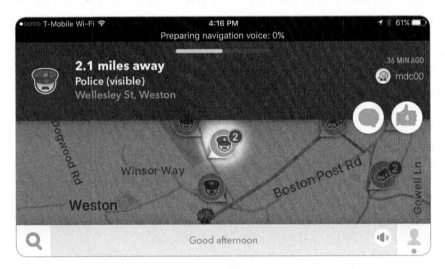

The app compiles location and speed reports from connected drivers. These reports are used to identify traffic jams and other slowdowns. Users can actively submit reports to Waze, too, using the big Waze button and colorful icons for common hazards. While it's helpful to warn other drivers of obstacles, it's not worth getting into an accident, so don't fiddle with the app while the car is in motion.

Another issue with Waze: It's a power hog. Plug the phone into a charger in your car if you are using Waze for more than 30 minutes.

Conclusion, and a request

Thanks for reading *iPhone Basics In 30 Minutes*. I have tried to make this a helpful introduction to the iPhone and its powerful hardware and software features. I haven't covered everything, however, so be sure to explore the many apps and other features.

Online, there is a companion website that contains more information about the phone, as well as blog posts, app reviews, and videos. The site is located at *iphone.in30minutes.com*. There are also links to other resources mentioned in this book, including *Dropbox In 30 Minutes*. If you have a specific question that was not answered in the book, feel free to contact me at *ian@ in30minutes.com* or on Twitter (@ilamont).

Lastly, if you have a few minutes to spare, I would greatly appreciate it if you could leave a short review online. Your honest opinions not only let other people know what to expect, but they also raise the profile of the book. I don't have the same marketing resources as the big publishing houses, so every review counts.

Thanks again for reading!

Index

Notes

Notes

Notes

Notes

CPSIA information can be obtained
at www.ICGtesting.com
Printed in the USA
LVOW13s1617250117

522153LV00011B/1237/P